Praise for *Fast Fiction*

"*Fast Fiction* is filled with stellar advice, solid-gold tips, and doable, practical exercises for all writers who want to draft a complete novel."

— Melissa Walker, author of *Violet on the Runway*

"Being a 'pantser' I have always resisted outlining, but I have to say that *Fast Fiction* changed my mind! Denise Jaden takes what I find to be a scary process (outlining) and makes it into an easy and, dare I say, enjoyable one. *Fast Fiction* is a hands-on book that asks the right questions to get your mind and your story flowing. I know I'll be using *Fast Fiction* over and over again. Highly recommended for fiction writers!"

— Janet Gurtler, author of RITA Award finalist *I'm Not Her*

"*Fast Fiction* is full of strategies and insights that will inspire and motivate writers of every experience level — and best of all, it provides them with a solid plan to quickly complete the first draft of their next novel."
— Mindi Scott, author of *Freefall*

"*Fast Fiction* provides writers with the perfect mix of practical guidance and the kick in the pants they need to finish that draft. This book is a must-have for writers of all levels."

— Eileen Cook, author of *The Almost Truth*

"Practical and down-to-earth, Denise Jaden's *Fast Fiction* makes a one-month draft seem doable, even for beginners, any month of the year."

— Jennifer Echols, author of *Endless Summer* and *Playing Dirty*

"One of the greatest challenges any writer faces is getting a great idea out of one's brain and onto the page. *Fast Fiction* breaks that process down into concrete, manageable steps, each accompanied by Denise

Jaden's sage advice and enthusiastic encouragement. And anything that helps streamline the drafting process is a-okay by me! *Fast Fiction* is a great addition to any writer's toolbox — I've got it in mine!"
    — Catherine Knutsson, author of *Shadows Cast by Stars*

"Forget the fact that this resource is directed at those wanting to complete a fast draft — if you're out to get your novel done, period, Jaden's *Fast Fiction* will be the kick in the butt that gets you there, from story plan to 'The End'…and beyond."
    — Judith Graves, author of the Skinned series for young adults

FAST FICTION

Also by Denise Jaden

Never Enough

Losing Faith

Writing with a Heavy Heart

FAST
FICTION

A Guide to Outlining and Writing a First-Draft Novel in Thirty Days

DENISE JADEN

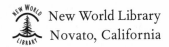
New World Library
Novato, California

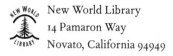
New World Library
14 Pamaron Way
Novato, California 94949

Text design by Tona Pearce Myers

Library of Congress Cataloging-in-Publication Data is available.

First printing, March 2014
ISBN 978-1-60868-254-6
Printed in the USA on 100% postconsumer-waste recycled paper

New World Library is proud to be a Gold Certified Environmentally Responsible Publisher. Publisher certification awarded by Green Press Initiative. www.greenpressinitiative.org

10 9 8 7 6 5 4 3 2 1

To Shana Silver,
who introduced me to fast-drafting, to outlining,
and to NaNoWriMo

CONTENTS

Introduction   xiii

Part One: Before the Draft

1. The Story Idea   3
2. Plot and the Three-Act Structure   9
3. The Characters   25
4. Theme   47
5. Setting   51
6. Symbols, Images, and Icons   59
7. List of Scenes   63
8. Story Plan   69
9. How to Write a Fast Draft   73

Part Two: During the Draft

Days 1–7: Launching In

Day 1   87
Day 2   91

Day 3   94
Day 4   98
Day 5   101
Day 6   103
Day 7   106

Days 8–14: A New Direction

Day 8   109
Day 9   113
Day 10   115
Day 11   118
Day 12   120
Day 13   122
Day 14   124

Days 15–22: Deepen the Plot

Day 15   127
Day 16   130
Day 17   132
Day 18   134
Day 19   137
Day 20   139
Day 21   142
Day 22   145

Days 23–30: Race to the Finish

Day 23   147
Day 24   150
Day 25   153

Day 26   156

Day 27   158

Day 28   160

Day 29   162

Day 30   164

The Basic Plan (Cheat Sheet)   167

Part Three: After the Draft

Revision Techniques   171

Additional Resources   187

Acknowledgments   191

About the Author   193

INTRODUCTION

If someone had told me during my early writing days that I would be able to write a draft of an entire book in less than a month, I probably would have thought they were crazy. At the time, I took between one and two years to come up with a first draft, and even with that amount of time spent on those drafts, my early books were riddled with major plot problems.

In the fall of 2007, my critique partner, Shana Silver, introduced me to National Novel Writing Month, or NaNoWriMo (www.nanowrimo.org). It's a yearly challenge in which hundreds of thousands of writers around the world spur each other on to write a 50,000-word novel within the month of November.

I'll admit, I was more than skeptical. But with the help of my critique partner, I worked on an outline ahead of time and then jumped in with both feet on November 1. By November 21, I had a completed manuscript, which would go on to surpass my earlier novels (which had taken years to write) and become my first published novel, with Simon & Schuster (*Losing Faith* in 2010).

Needless to say, I was thrilled. I've been completing the "NaNo" challenge every year since, plus holding my own "March Madness" challenge yearly on my blog (denisejaden .blogspot.com). I've been honing my fast-drafting skills — learning what works and what doesn't — and I have some insight to share with you on the subject.

Most recently, I wrote one complete manuscript in November 2012, and a completely different one during the following month of March, and those will hopefully be my next two published books. They have been by far the fastest path from first draft to polished draft for me.

I've put together all my advice here in one book, along with writing prompts, free-writing exercises, and a day-by-day plan to take you through your month-long fast-drafting journey. This guide can be used as a companion to November's NaNo-WriMo, or it can be used at any time during the year when you would like to write a draft of a novel quickly.

My challenge to you is to write a novel in thirty days. Not in the next thirty days because we have some prep work to do first. But once you have your storywriting tools in hand, I'll set you loose to write about 2,000 words every day for thirty days.

I know that sounds daunting, but anyone can do this. I'm serious. There are only two key ingredients:

Diligence

Perseverance

Some would argue a third ingredient is skill, but I believe if you have enough diligence and perseverance, and if you follow a guide rather than writing aimlessly, skill will grow over time.

Some people are born storytellers. They can write a story

organically, by the seat of their pants, and it works. But anyone can develop their writing skills and learn the ingredients of good storytelling. In this book, I'll help you come up with a workable story plan ahead of time, check what's not working, and fix it before you pour too much blood, sweat, and tears into the idea.

Then, as you write each day during the month, I'll give you lots of hints about good storytelling and supply simple tasks to work into your manuscript. Hopefully each one will show up exactly when you need it. However, consider these tasks more as a set of prompts to get you going than an actual formula. They are meant to provide jumping-off places as well as the inspiration to push through even on the days when you feel like your muse has left the building. It's not that These-Steps-in-This-Order-Will-Give-You-a-Great-Book, but ideally, they will help you develop a richer story, giving it layers and momentum.

Indeed, one word of caution: This is not a get-rich-quick formula. This process is about fast-drafting a *first* draft, not a *polished* draft. You're not going to write a bestselling novel in a month, but you will have a complete first draft that you can make a clear judgment about. You'll have a finished product that you can put aside and then come back to and reevaluate with renewed perspective. Characters can take much longer than thirty days to truly understand and deliver to your readers. Some of my fast drafts have gone through so many later revisions that I've practically written the book again from scratch. By developing some of the techniques in this guide, and doing a little legwork before starting to fast-draft, I'm learning to avoid those extreme revisions.

This book's method focuses on learning by doing. During

my early days of writing, I read plenty of writing craft books, and I can't tell you how many times I read the phrase "show, don't tell." But you know what? I still wrote most of the time in narrative "telling" mode. Because I didn't get it. I didn't truly understand what "show, don't tell" meant until a critique partner pointed out within my own writing how I could take the reader right into the life of my character rather than explaining his actions from the outside.

Through this kinesthetic learning, you'll see your writing improve before your eyes. And if you stick with it to the end, you'll also enjoy the pride of accomplishment. At the end of your month, you'll be able to tell your friends that you wrote an entire novel. What will they say they did — watch TV?

Of course, no one fast-drafts to impress others. You do it for yourself, not for anyone else. So, if you have a passion to write, write about your passion. The heart of your story should reflect the heart of who you are. Ultimately, what truths do you want your story to convey? That's what we're about to find out. Remember, if you are passionate about your story, your reader is much more likely to follow.

So, where do you start?

Well, you could just jump in with an empty page, but that's not the approach I use. Instead, to keep your mojo revved up and turning its wheels throughout your month of writing, I recommend having a plan to work from, and part 1 will guide you in developing that plan. However, don't start planning *too* far ahead. I recommend carving out some planning time about one month before you want to start fast-drafting. You can certainly cram all your planning into the week before drafting if that's all you can manage, but I suggest committing to a few hours each week over the next four weeks. Keep your notebook handy through the whole month. When ideas start to flow, you'll want to be able to jot them down. Sometimes ideas need time to simmer, in order to become fully rounded. Planning a month ahead, you'll have enough time to get on a roll and develop all kinds of world-changing ideas, but not so much time that you'll become bored or, worse, start to second-guess your own best ideas.

The day-by-day section (part 2) will help you write a fast draft of a 50,000-word novel in thirty days. This section is not intended to be read ahead of time. Once you've begun, simply open to the day of the month that you're on, read the inspirational story and tidbits of advice, and launch into that day's writing. Part 3 is a short section on revision, in which I'll give you lots of ideas on how to take your fast draft and turn it into a polished draft. Don't worry, you'll get a nice long break before you even have to look at that.

This book will act as a guide to brainstorming and collecting your ideas into a usable plan, and then the daily inspirations will help you quickly take that plan to a written first draft of a full novel.

I look forward to hearing of your success at fast-drafting!

Onward, Fearless Writers...

Part One

BEFORE THE DRAFT

Chapter One

THE STORY IDEA

Where do you get inspiration for story ideas? Mine come from all sorts of different sources. Sometimes I'll be watching a movie, and in the first five minutes I start to speculate on where the movie is going and how it'll end. Usually it moves in a completely different direction, so I'm left with a cool story idea all my own.

Sometimes I wake up in the morning with the remnants of a dream in my head. That can be the spark of a great story idea.

I also get ideas from talking with friends about things they've done or people they know, or events that have happened in my own life. Many authors take their story ideas straight from newspaper headlines.

Plot ideas can come from almost anywhere. The important thing is to keep your eyes and ears open. Pay attention to the people, events, settings, and stories that interest *you*.

If you have trouble coming up with good story ideas, don't worry. Chances are, you have many of them already stored in the back reaches of your brain. To access these ideas, practice brainstorming. Brainstorming is a simple but effective skill that you'll need as a writer.

Here are some guidelines for brainstorming:

1. There are no hard-and-fast rules.
2. There are no bad ideas.
3. Your instincts are more important than you usually give them credit for.
4. Dream big and wild.
5. Use free writing and writing prompts when you're stuck.

With free writing, set a time limit for yourself — five minutes or an hour, whatever you can handle — and write without stopping. Write down whatever comes into your mind, even if it's just "I don't know what to write." The process of writing will eventually get your creative juices flowing. Writing prompts, on the other hand, give you a starting place, something to springboard off of. Whether you're free writing or using prompts, I recommend pushing yourself to keep your pen (or keyboard) in constant motion throughout the time you have set for yourself. Sometimes you'll need to write through a few repetitive or boring ideas in order to get to the really good ideas.

When brainstorming, relax for a few minutes before you start and let your mind wander. I guarantee ideas will appear and start to spark your interest. Jot them down loosely, without trying to shape them. Does a certain type of person, job, or circumstance seem intriguing, amusing, or shocking? Write it down and launch from that into your free writing. This can be a seed from which you grow your plot.

So, your first task before fast-drafting is to spend twenty minutes brainstorming as many character, event, and story ideas as you can think of. Sometimes you may prefer to do this on a computer, but today I recommend the old-school pen (or pencil) and paper method. The motion of handwriting, as well as the time it takes to get the words down on paper, can allow your mind to really explore your creative ideas. Plus, studies suggest that the act of forming letters may help with memory, ideas, and expression.

I recommend keeping a notebook with you at all times. You never know when ideas will strike. In fact, I keep an app on my iPhone called "A Novel Idea." It's free, and it's a great place to make plotting and/or character notes.

Come back to your brainstorming a day or two later and circle anything that can be formed into story ideas — that is, anything to do with characters and character relationships, their motivations and desires, or obstacles. Complete as many brainstorming sessions as you need in order to get a list of at least ten circled ideas. Write these on a separate piece of paper and add any details you can think of for each one.

For example, maybe one of your ideas is about an abusive marital relationship. Can you picture either of the spouses? Write down whatever you envision. Which one is abused? What does that character want? Which one is the abuser? What does that character want? Can you think of any obstacles that are getting in the way of what either of these characters want?

Once you've jotted down some notes on all your ideas, choose a few of the ones that grab you the most to craft into short one- or two-sentence premise statements. A premise is the basic central idea, circumstance, or dilemma of your story; you will build your plot from this. You could combine numerous brainstorming ideas into a single premise, but it's good practice to trim each one into a single sentence. This is handy when you're sharing and explaining your writing with friends, and it's essential when it comes time to market your story to publishing professionals.

As an example, let's look at a few premises many of you will recognize:

A young girl gets stranded in a strange new land and sets off on a dangerous journey to meet the one person who has the power to send her home.

Do you recognize this premise? I purposely made the description a little vague, to show how the same premise might fit a variety of stories, but it's *The Wizard of Oz*.

Or try this one:

A suicidal family man gets a glimpse of the world as it would be if he hadn't been born.

This is the basic premise of *It's a Wonderful Life*.

Here's one more:

An old miser is visited by three ghosts who remind him of the spirit of Christmas.

I'll bet you guessed that this one is from *A Christmas Carol*.

Here is the one-line story idea I started with for my latest work-in-progress young adult novel, *Tent*:

Wild-child Delaney Peters attempts to punk a religious tent meeting but instead starts experiencing strange and increasingly embarrassing miracles.

We'll come back to that premise, and I'll show you how I expanded it to grow a fully formed novel.

Once you have a solid premise statement (if you have several, pick the one that pulls at you the most), spend some time thinking about genre, audience, and setting. Are you going to write your story for children or adults? Is it going to be a mystery or an action-adventure or have gory moments that will make even the strongest stomach turn? Will it be set in the past, present, or future? Will it have otherworldly elements or will characters live in the real world?

Whatever you decide, it is important to nail down one or two main genres that your novel will work into.

Here are some common fiction genres in professional publishing:

Contemporary
Drama
Dystopian
Erotica
Fantasy
Futuristic
Historical
Horror
Humor
Literary
Mystery
Paranormal
Realistic
Romance
Science Fiction
Western

If you approach your story like it's something brand new that cannot be categorized, it may make you feel like a pioneer of publishing, but it could be more difficult to create a satisfying plot arc, to connect with readers who are used to established genres, and to get your story published traditionally.

Again, before you start to plot your story, I encourage you to wrangle your idea into a concise sentence. Your premise statement may change over time, of course, but the more you can harness your ideas and keep them in tight, quick-glance form, the more easily you can make use of them in your story plan.

Chapter Two

PLOT AND THE THREE-ACT STRUCTURE

What is plot? Even if you can't explain it in concise terms, I'll bet you know right away if it's missing from a book or movie! How many times have you found yourself shaking your head, saying, "I don't get it. What is this story about, anyway?"

Plot is the structure or framework on which you hang your story. Plots vary, but when planning for your fast draft, I want you to focus on imagining your story in three main parts: First, define a problem or a quest. Then, describe the obstacles that get in the way of solving the problem or continuing the quest. Finally, in some form, resolve the problem, or complete the quest, ideally in a way that involves growth and self-revelation for your main character. This always makes the most satisfying plot.

Or, to put it into one sentence: Create a plot in which a character wants something, but there are obstacles in the way, and the character has to pay a cost and/or change in some way to get what's desired.

This three-act structure comes straight from screenwriting or movie script instruction. With script writing, the parameters are very specific in what professionals are looking for, and oddly enough, these parameters work well for novel writing, too, even down to the number of pages you spend on each stage. Though movie scripts are shorter than novel manuscripts (say, around 120 double-spaced pages for a movie compared to 300 pages for an average novel), you would be smart to work within the same proportionate guidelines — with shorter beginnings and endings and a longer middle. The middle typically includes lots of twists and turns (with several obstacles to overcome), while the beginning should have punch and the ending should quicken the momentum as the story climaxes and finishes.

Plotting a Three-Act Roller Coaster

Now, take your one-sentence premise and, using the brainstorming ideas in this chapter, spend some time expanding that with events and scenes that fit the scope of that premise. What might happen, and how might things play out? Even if you're unsure, jot down any ideas that come to you. Do not leave any idea unwritten!

Remember my one-line premise from *Tent*: Wild-child Delaney Peters attempts to punk a religious tent meeting but instead starts experiencing strange and increasingly embarrassing miracles.

In this case, I started brainstorming with scenes that could happen at a tent meeting, different settings and embarrassing situations where miracles could take place, and what would drive my main character to want to punk a tent meeting in the first place.

With your premise sentence in front of you, keep coming

up with as many ideas as you can and see how they might fit together. Even if certain ideas don't end up playing a part in your fast-draft novel, ideas spring from ideas, so don't be afraid to write anything down. Often our *aha* moments come not from suddenly getting "the right" idea, but from seeing *connections* between ideas that you hadn't seen before.

Again, write everything down that comes to mind! You may want a separate notebook for this.

Then, to arrange your story into the three-act structure, your first section should introduce the main characters and give only the *essential* setting and background information. Most importantly, it should feature an "inciting incident" — that is, the first moment when things change and cannot go back to the way they were for your main character. I'll talk about this more below.

Your middle includes subplots that help your reader get to know your characters more fully. The middle should keep your characters active and busy. Often, meeting challenges sends your main character in a whole new direction — probably the wrong direction.

Your ending is all about tying things up neatly — but not too neatly.

Here is a quickie formula for planning the amount of material in each stage and for how much time to spend when you're fast-drafting:

Act I: Beginning — About the first 50 pages of a novel
    (days 1–7 of drafting)
Act II: Middle — The middle 200 pages of a novel
    (days 8–23 of drafting)
Act III: Ending — The last 50 pages (days 24–30 of
    drafting)

NaNoWriMo's *Young Writers' Program Workbook* suggests it might help to think of the plot of your story like a roller coaster. Here's one way to do so:

Act I: The Setup

This introduces your protagonist, his or her want or desire, and a possible obstacle to that want. All this can feel like climbing the first big hill of a roller coaster. Your inciting incident should hit by page 50 (or sooner), and this will feel like the crest of the first big hill — the moment from which your protagonist cannot or will not turn back.

Act II: The Middle

This is the longest section of your book — say, 200 pages — and it should build character development and tension toward the eventual climax. Think of it like all the fun little twists and turns, the hills and valleys, in the middle of the roller coaster. They are the fun parts that don't quite scare the pants off you.

Act III: The Climax and Resolution

This section should be about the same length as the beginning, 50 pages. It's the moment in your book when your readers will hold their breath, needing resolution. Think of this like rounding the peak of the roller coaster's highest, biggest hill — when you know the plunge is coming! Then comes the fast-paced falling action. After that last big hill, the story should maintain that fast, thrilling pace all the way until it makes it back to the station for the final resolution. The resolution answers two questions:

Does your protagonist get what he or she wanted or not? Either way, how is the character forever changed?

A Sample Three-Act Synopsis

By the time you're ready to fast-draft, you should be able to describe the essence of what is planned for each act in one short paragraph.

Here are three brief paragraphs describing *The Wizard of Oz*, so you get the idea:

In act I, we meet Dorothy, the main character, and see her in her normal world of Kansas, where she's unsatisfied in her life. The dissatisfaction is bearable until her dog, Toto, is confiscated. A tornado swoops into Dorothy's life and transports her to the world of Oz.

Some may say the tornado is the inciting incident, or the moment from which Dorothy's life is forever changed. But since her dog is so important to her, and losing him ultimately brings out the side of her that would stay outside and face a tornado, I would consider the loss of Toto as the inciting incident.

In act II, Dorothy meets her antagonist, the Wicked Witch. She takes a journey to lead her home and meets three secondary characters, each with his own plight, along her path. She finally makes it to the Wizard, who is supposed to get her home, but a complication occurs: the Wizard requires Dorothy to fetch the witch's broomstick before he will help her.

Act III begins when things are at their worst, and Dorothy is locked up in the witch's chamber. Her friends help her escape and overtake the witch, but even with the witch's broom, the Wizard is unable to get her home. With help, Dorothy realizes that she has had the power to get herself home all along.

Character Motivation

One key to creating a successful three-act structure is figuring out your main character's driving motivation. The character may want and desire many things, but one central desire should run throughout the book. To figure this out, brainstorm and list all the things each character you've considered so far might want, big or small, and circle the ones that you think could be important, story-carrying wants.

This list could include almost anything. A character might want...

   ...to get into the best college.
   ...to date a newcomer at school.
   ...to be promoted within the police force.
   ...to become a famous chef.
   ...to find a missing child, and so on.

Every character in your book should have multiple wants and desires. This will help them feel human, since everyone has wants and desires. This will also give you more fodder for conflict, which, in turn, will give your story momentum. Your characters' motivation and believability will spring from how strong their wants and desires are and how well they are conveyed for the reader. Your characters' actions will only be believable to your reader if the reader believes in those characters' desires.

For each of your planned characters (and you should come back to this stage as you come up with new characters), list at least three wants or desires. Don't worry about how they'll fit into the plot just yet. Simply brainstorm motivations.

Now let's talk a little bit about need.

Creating characters with multiple wants and desires is great. It's even better when those wants and desires conflict with one another. But your main character should also have one desire that's greater than all the rest and that carries through the book. The character should *need* something. There has to be something essential at stake. In other words, for the main character, ask why each desire is important, and what will happen if the character doesn't fulfill it.

For example, say your main character is a woman whose driving need is to pay a backlog of rent. What will happen if she can't? As you answer this question, keep raising the stakes; really catastrophize the situation. Maybe her landlord will stalk her and interrupt her at her job. Maybe he'll threaten to reveal a secret or ruin her life in some way. Maybe she knows he's a mobster, and she fears being beaten in a dark alley or even killed if she doesn't come up with the money.

The more drastic the stakes, the more motivated your character will be, and the more your reader will be invested. Look at your list of characters and their wants: could some be made stronger so they are actually needs? In fact, it's useful simply to make a list of things someone could need. Whether you use these ideas in the book you're currently mapping out or not, this list will remain useful for all later books. In essence, this could be any situation with life-or-death, or at least life-altering, consequences. Here are a few examples:

- Your character is the only one who can save someone from being killed or from taking his or her own life.
- Your character is suddenly abandoned by a lover or spouse and needs to know why.

- Your character falls in love with someone forbidden and needs to win over the person, and possibly everyone else in the person's life.
- Someone important to your character dies or is taken away. How will the character survive without that person?

Start with Questions, Not Incidents

One mistake many writers make when outlining their novels is trying too hard to find the inciting incident, or the first moment when the story's action truly begins. This will come, and it will feel more organic if you let it emerge as you're working through your story during planning, rather than trying to force an inciting incident up front.

A better approach to working out the beginning of your story is to give your reader questions to ask. The moment your main character appears, the reader should be asking questions, such as, why is the character so sad or angry or happy? What will the character do with a certain object? What kind of moral decision is the character about to make, and what will the consequences be?

Treat each book as a mystery, even if it isn't one. Pepper in questions for the reader, and always leave some questions unanswered while steadily raising new questions for the character and your reader.

Any aspect of your story can be used to raise questions — the history of different characters and their relationships, hidden motivations and other secrets. Minor questions might be answered within the first scene, such as, "Will his mom notice he's lying?" Other questions should be larger and related to the motivations that will run throughout the book, such as, "Does the guy she's in love with have feelings for her, too?" However, whether they are big or small, questions should arise for your reader and/or your main character right from the first paragraph.

Questions are what motivate readers to turn the page. They may even motivate you to write the next page. Questions propel your novel forward and give it momentum. So, before deciding on your inciting incident, list some of the questions you want your reader to ask about your main characters right at the beginning of your story, such as who they are, what they are feeling, why they are acting in certain ways, and what they want.

Obstacles, Subplots, and Complexity

Now that you've brainstormed the material that will become your novel's opening — your main characters and their motivating needs, wants, and questions — consider all the possible challenges they could face and list them. This list should include the following.

- Obstacles to every main need for all characters in your story. For example, what is stopping your character from getting into the best college?
- Character conflicts or traits that clash. Perhaps one of your characters is a pessimist, while another is an optimist.
- Settings that present specific difficulties. Maybe your character's child disappears in the middle of busy, crowded New York City.
- Changing desires or unexpected turns of fortune. What if your main character loved his well-paying job until the company he works for was sold?

This list of obstacles and challenges might get long, and that's fine. Most novel-length books need more than just a single plotline to propel the story along. One of my favorite questions to ask is: "How can my story be more complex?" It's a good question to ask regularly.

So, consider if some of the character challenges might be developed into subplots. While having subplots isn't strictly necessary, they often can be used to support the main story and make it more interesting and complex. They add depth to secondary characters and to the world where the story takes place. Subplots are not their own stories, but rather expertly woven additions to the main story. However, sometimes authors will take a subplot from one book and expand it into its own book — as a companion novel or a sequel.

Imagine a braid, where the center strand is the main plotline and the outside strands are subplots. As you structure your story, the subplots should be not completely separate stories but rather stories that are twisted around the main plot to create a tight braid.

A great way to come up with subplots is to consider your secondary characters and your antagonist. What are *their* stories and backgrounds, and could their stories add flavor or complications to the main plotline? Do any of their wants and desires clash with your main character's wants? Do they have needs that could launch separate stories parallel to the main one? Think of the three characters Dorothy runs into along the yellow brick road in *The Wizard of Oz*. They each have their own desires and obstacles, yet their stories work well alongside Dorothy's quest.

As you brainstorm possible subplots, be aware that adding any subplots may be too ambitious during a thirty-day fast draft. When it comes time to fast-draft, use whatever your story needs to build the main plot, and perhaps leave yourself notes about developing certain subplots during revisions later. Of course, if a subplot emerges organically during your thirty days, go with it, but don't feel like it's something you need to have. Remember, you have to tie up all the loose ends by the end of your story, including all subplots.

Certainly, as you begin fast-drafting for the first time, start with one main character and tell his or her story in a linear, chronological way. Start at the beginning and move forward in time. Stay focused on your main plot thread in order to finish the story by the end of your thirty days.

Keep Characters Active, Not Passive

While plotting your story, remember to keep your main character active. Though things will of course happen *to* your character, you want your protagonist to be actively engaged as much as possible.

For instance, perhaps your character is a teenager who has her car stolen. What's the most active response? Having her accept it and go home? Having her call the police and let them handle it? Or having her jump onto a motorcycle and hunt down the thief? Now *that* would be interesting to read about!

In other words, the plot is made up of all the ways your main character is actively trying to solve his or her main need, dilemma, or question. What the character does, not all that happens around or to the character, makes the plot happen.

Pulling the Plot Together

Actions and events make up the basic structure of your story. Questions and reveals at optimal times create page-turning tension. All events in your story should include new information that either helps or hinders your main character on his or her journey.

Now that you've spent time brainstorming some elements of your plot, including the wants, needs, questions, and obstacles for your main characters, further divide them and add them to your three-act structure. How will these play into the beginning, middle, and end of your book? As you map out what you know so far, is the plot becoming clearer? If there are gaps and holes, write what you *do* know and try to brainstorm the missing pieces, or leave your three-act outline for a few days and come back to it.

In particular, consider what might make a good launching-off place for your story, and what might make a good resolution at the end. If your main character needs her soul mate, will she get him? Or, like Dorothy in *The Wizard of Oz*, will she realize that what she really needs is within herself?

Choosing Your Inciting Incident

As I've said, your story should have an event or incident that changes things for the main character right near the beginning. Think of what this event could be. It could be the thing that causes your story's main need, such as someone close to the character going missing or dying, the character flunking an important exam, the character getting pregnant, and so on.

This inciting incident should create forward momentum. Can your main character return to how things were in his or her "before world"? If so, you have not thought of your inciting incident yet. Your inciting incident will propel your main character forward, bring sympathy from the reader, and make the stakes for your character clear. The inciting incident should be rife with conflict and grab the reader's attention. It's usually followed by action, since it is such a life-changing moment that your character now has to *do* something about this new situation.

Your inciting incident should occur within the first quarter of the book, but during fast-drafting, you can be flexible. If you realize while drafting that it appears later, it probably just means that you've included too much buildup and backstory at the beginning. Most likely, this is either unnecessary or can be moved to later in your novel, which you can figure out during revisions (see part 3).

If you still don't really understand what an inciting incident is, I recommend you watch a few movies with these questions in mind: At what point is the main character unable to return to his or her normal life? Why? What happened to change things?

The inciting incident does not have to look huge and glamorous. For instance, in the movie *The Breakfast Club,* the inciting incident is very subtle. To me, it is the moment when the popular girl, Claire, covers for rebellious Bender when he takes the screw out of the door. How do things change after that moment? Bender knows he can take this group in a new direction. Once the most popular of them has covered for him once, he knows he can make any of them do anything with enough leadership and persuasion.

Apply this to your own story. At what point will your main character be unable to return to his or her previous life? At what point will the situation change in a way that cannot be reversed?

Handling Backstory

When drafting a novel, writers have a tendency to ramble near the beginning, spending too much time on setup and backstory rather than jumping right into the actual story. It's a temptation that's easy to understand: you spend a lot of time imagining the lives of your characters, and you want to include those details in your book. You want your readers to understand every nuance about the characters you have created. The problem is, your reader may not care about the details and background of a character who is new to him until he's become invested in that character's plight.

Once you have a good idea of what your inciting incident is, consider carefully how much setup you need beforehand. What would the story be missing if you jumped right into the inciting incident and came back later to reveal your main character's backstory?

In essence, backstory is simply all the details from your characters' lives that came *before* the main story. How you work them into your story usually varies: sometimes these are peppered in with tiny comments; at other times they are fully played out in the form of flashbacks. Whatever the case, backstory has a fairly bad reputation in the writing world due to its misuse or overuse. But just because it is hard to handle well, please don't be tempted to throw it out the window altogether. Backstory, properly placed, can deepen the conflict and characterization in your story, plus it will be a useful tool to help you explore your characters' world while drafting a new novel.

So be warned: it's quite likely that you will end up with too much backstory in the early parts of your first draft. That's okay! It's part of the process of getting to know your characters and of developing an organic-feeling world. During revision, you can trim or resituate your backstory as necessary, so don't hold back during your first draft. If you have important information about your characters that your readers need to know, include it. Just be prepared for a little shuffling around later.

Midstory Reversals and Subplots

For the middle section, can you think of at least one way that your main character can be taken in the wrong direction, or one obstacle that will send the character farther from his or her goal? Reversals and obstacles help to show what your character is made of. Even if your character unknowingly heads in the wrong direction, farther from his or her goal, you want your reader to have added respect for the character's motivation and tenacity, for the willingness to try *something* in order to reach his or her goals.

Obstacles should truly challenge your characters. Each obstacle that is overcome should make your characters stronger in the reader's eyes, and should add page-turning tension. The best obstacles and reversals will relate directly to your main character's needs in the story.

Think of the roller coaster analogy and include as many twists and turns as possible here. Are there secondary characters whose subplots can become more prominent? How can you show conflicting desires between your main character and some of your secondary characters?

Drafting a Three-Act Synopsis

Once you've made lists and notes for each stage of your story, try to write one short paragraph for each act: the beginning, middle, and end. Include answers to the questions I ask above. Don't worry if you're not feeling a strong sense of where your story is going yet. We have plenty more preparation to do before we get to the writing stage. For now, just keep jotting down your ideas and circling the best ones or the ones you feel most passionately about, and keep revisiting the three-act outline as your ideas become clearer.

Your plot may be simple at first, but it should always be growing in complexity. One small problem or conflict makes for a weak story. One big conflict, plus several small ones, makes for a much more engaging story. So don't hold back on your ideas. You may use five of them or you may use a hundred.

Chapter Three

THE CHARACTERS

Do you usually start planning your stories with a focus on plot or character? If you are like me, then you probably think of interesting characters first. The way my mind works, I tend to get a couple of characters in my mind, I develop a relationship between them, and then the plot of the story grows out of my understanding of their relationship.

For instance, with my first two young adult novels, my initial ideas had to do with the relationship between two sisters. As I got to know the sisters, I started to understand possible problems they might have, not only with each other, but also with their surrounding world. This understanding, in turn, helped me realize what the main obstacles in their lives would be, and out of this grew a plot for a novel.

In this chapter, I will help you fully develop your characters so they will feel real and be engaging for the reader. If this leads you to rethink your plot, or any other aspect of your story so far, then go back and make the necessary changes. Keep everything as loose as possible right now.

The characters in your story will fall into three general categories:

Protagonist — the main character(s). The story is usually told from or through his or her point(s) of view.
Antagonist — a character who opposes the protagonist.
Secondary characters — the supporting cast of the
novel.

Using these categories, list all the characters you are currently planning for your story. Be as comprehensive and inclu-
sive as possible. Don't worry about names just yet; we'll get to
that below.

Then, before diving into your own characters fully, spend
some time pondering fictional characters you've already met in
books and movies:

1.   What are some reasons you bond with characters in a
      book or movie? What might make readers bond with
      your main character?
2.   What are some reasons you dislike characters? Who are
      some of the characters you've disliked? Were you meant
      to dislike them, or were they badly conceived? Would
      you have liked them more if they had more positive attri-
      butes or were more well-rounded or more "human"?
3.   Who are the most memorable fictional characters you've
      ever encountered, and what makes these characters mem-
      orable?
4.   What qualities make characters seem realistic to you?

Deep characters, like people, are multifaceted. They do and
say the unexpected. To be realistic, characters need believable
motivations, and they need flaws — even the hunky, brutish
love interest needs a good flaw or two.

Point of View

By this point, you probably already know who your main character is, and perhaps even whose point of view you will write your story from. However, as you develop your characters in this chapter, keep the issue of point of view in mind and ask yourself: Is this really the head you want to be in and the voice you want to hear for 300 or more pages? Is there someone else who might be more interesting to read about or who has more at stake in this story? Also, will this be a story that's conveyed better in the first person, third person, or even perhaps second person?

First-person point of view (using first-person pronouns: "I did this, I did that") can be a handy way to write a first draft. It can help you really feel the things your main character feels. You have a front-row seat for your main character's thoughts, which are delivered directly to the reader.

First-person point of view also has drawbacks, as there are with any choice. In first-person point of view, you only get to deliver the thoughts and perspectives of the character whose head you are in. If most of the drama in your story concerns one main character and his or her inner turmoil, then first-person point of view could be the perfect choice. But if you have a complex cast and want the reader to see multiple points of view, if you want to bounce around in different characters' thoughts often, then first person might feel too limiting and simplistic.

If you choose first person, another issue to watch out for is the lack of development in secondary characters. In first-person narratives, writers spend so much time connecting with and practically becoming their main character that they can forget to fully develop the rest of their cast. One strategy to avoid this is to periodically change the first-person perspective as you write.

Third-person point of view (using third-person pronouns: "He did this, he did that") is another great choice. As the "omniscient narrator," you can choose how much you reveal of different characters and their points of view, which can add flexibility to how you tell your story. With third-person point of view you can decide how transparent you'd like to be with your characters' thought processes. You can still tell the story mainly from one person's point of view, while shifting to address multiple points of view. During fast-drafting, one drawback to using third person is that it can be a little more difficult or time-consuming to really connect with your main characters and their voices. Also, if you're telling a story in multiple points of view, that can be a large undertaking for a thirty-day draft.

Finally, second-person point of view (using second-person pronouns: "you did this, you did that") is a more unusual technique with which to tell a story. Typically, it mimics an observer addressing the story's main protagonist, or it's when the narrator addresses the reader directly. If you are new to fast-drafting, I recommend sticking to first- or third-person point of view, but that doesn't mean you can't use second person if you're comfortable with it.

Creating Likable Main Characters

Likable or sympathetic characters are usually those characters that portray the characteristics we wish we had. They are smarter, wittier, tougher, kinder, more focused, more talented, and often more selfless than we are.

Here are a few things that can help make your protagonist likable:

- A positive attitude. Who wants to read about someone who's complaining or grumpy all the time?
- A great sense of humor. Yes, funny can be difficult to write, but the good news is, unlike when having a conversation with a friend, you have as long as you need to come up with witty lines and banter. Later, you can edit your jokes until they are seamless. Also, having a great sense of humor doesn't necessarily mean the character is witty all the time, just good-humored and not easily offended.
- Willing to meet challenges. A likable character doesn't cower in the face of danger or difficulty.
- Exceeds expectations. Likable characters usually go the extra mile. They're not lazy or apathetic.
- Treats other characters (and animals) well. This can be especially effective when your character looks out for an underdog.
- Fearless. Many people live with fear, but we are always attracted to those who don't seem to be afraid of anything.
- Calm. In the midst of panic, a calm and steady character is admirable.
- Driven toward a goal. If your character desperately wants something, your reader will want it, too.

All that said, perfect or near-perfect characters are no fun to read about. They lack believability and depth. Every character needs flaws and weaknesses, just as every person has flaws and weaknesses. Perhaps your main character is extremely funny, but he has no control over his spending and is constantly scrimping to buy groceries for his family. Or maybe your main character can't help taking in every stray animal in sight, but when it comes to people, she has trouble opening up and trusting.

So, first brainstorm and list your main character's various strengths, and then list your main character's biggest weaknesses. Some attributes will stand out more than others. Circle those. You don't have to narrow his or her attributes down to only one or two. Some characters, like some of us, have many flaws!

With these attributes in mind, consider what your character needs at this point in his or her life. I asked you to brainstorm about this earlier, and now we can narrow it down further. How can you make that need even stronger? Need and desire will help your reader be on your character's side. Spend some time thinking of how you can make this need not just important but crucial to your character.

Consider giving your main characters a variety of physical *and* emotional needs, so they are more layered and complex. Perhaps the father in your story not only needs to find his missing daughter but needs to feel useful so he won't be suicidal.

What will be your main character's arc or change throughout the novel? I mentioned this in chapter two, when discussing developing your plot, but it bears repeating: When it comes to your main character, the primary thing to figure out is what major change the character will go through from the beginning of your novel to the end. Where will the character start, as what type of person and with what needs, and in what ways will the character grow the most?

A Hero's Journey

Your protagonist is more than just a main character. At a structural level in your story, he or she is your *hero*, or the one your reader will be engaged with and rooting for. Is he or she starting to take shape in your mind? Let's ponder ways of making this character even stronger and more engaging.

Who are your personal heroes?

Why? What qualities do these people have that you admire?

If they're not already included in the list of your main character's strengths, can you add any of these qualities to the hero you're creating?

For your character to embody this quality convincingly, you'll want to show evidence of it at least three times. Keep this in mind when we get to the point of outlining scenes, as it may help jump-start some scenes for you.

Heroes don't always have to be completely likable, but they do have to be larger than life. If you write about someone mundane, like your neighbor, readers are not going to want to read about him for 10 pages, let alone 300. Real people's lives are boring most of the time. Real people go to the store; they go to school and to work; they eat breakfast, lunch, and dinner. Everyday lives are just not that exciting to read about.

Multidimensional characters keep us guessing. If characters are easy to figure out, they are flat and boring to read about. It's what a character does that makes him or her a true hero, so take some time to envision how these new character strengths will play out in action throughout your story.

Simple Task: Voicing Your Hero

As a quick free-writing exercise, one that literary agent Donald Maass recommends in his books and workshops, try writing one paragraph in your main character's voice in a way that expresses his or her most prominent trait. Then write another paragraph in which the character expresses the opposite of that trait, in order to show the full range of depth to this character quality. If a character is generally fearless, show us what makes the person afraid. If a character is generally smart and quick-witted, show us what kind of situation would make the person bumble over his or her words. Really stretch yourself to find another believable but not-so-obvious side of your hero.

Does this deepen your understanding of your main character? Has this taught you anything new about him or her?

Creating Your Antagonist

An antagonist is someone who is opposed to or in conflict with the hero. That doesn't make the character a bad person. In fact, if your antagonist is all bad, the character won't be believable. At a minimum, the antagonist needs to believe he or she is doing the right thing, even if you and your main character don't.

But your antagonist does not have to be bad at all. It can often make a more powerful story if the antagonist actually wants something very good — but that something just happens to conflict with what your main character wants. This sort of conflict deepens the moral dilemma of your story, since it resists clear-cut answers, and this will deepen the reader's involvement. You want your reader to ponder what he or she would do in the same situation, and hopefully it won't be obvious.

No matter how good your antagonist is, however, keep in mind that the character's main narrative role is to keep your hero from reaching his or her goal, and the antagonist must do so for his or her own purposes — not just for yours. The stronger your antagonist is, the stronger your main character will seem for overcoming him or her. In other words, your antagonist can help make your main character into someone your readers will truly look up to and want to read about. Could you overcome the antagonist? If so, the character is probably not strong enough.

So, one important question to ask regarding your antagonist is: Why is the antagonist acting as an antagonist in *this* story and for *this* main character? What makes him or her "the one"? What characteristics does your antagonist possess that are like iron sharpening iron in relation to your main character?

What a Villain Wants

Your main character is usually your hero, but your antagonist does not have to be a villain. Sometimes your antagonist will be a morally upstanding character with altruistic goals. And that's great as long as he or she is a worthy opponent for your main character.

But sometimes your antagonist will be a villain. Villains will often have a negative effect on other characters besides your main character. They are often perceived as cruel or malicious in nature by readers and characters alike.

Good villains, though, like any strong character, are multidimensional. Even though they are the "bad guy" in the story, they must have wants, just like your main character, and just like you and me. They must also have some intentions they consider to be good, important, or necessary in order to feel realistic. The combination of their deep good intentions and their bad, angry, or evil actions can create some memorable villains.

Simple Task: The Villain's POV

Start by listing some of your favorite antagonists and villains from movies or books: What do you like most about these characters? What makes them "good" villains?

Now, rethink the movie or book from the villain's point of view. How would the story look and progress if told from that character's perspective? Make the antagonist's case — why *should* things go the villain's way? How would it change the plot for the antagonist to succeed?

Finally, consider the story you're planning: What if it was told from the antagonist's point of view? Could that point of view be included at some point? Take a few minutes and think about what the story would be like if it was your antagonist's story. This will give you greater insight into the character and his or her goals.

Creating Secondary Characters

Secondary characters are not unimportant. Secondary characters should set the stage for the main plot and the main characters. They bring your story to life and keep it running when your protagonist is having a down moment. Make them well-developed, fully realized people, too. For each secondary character in your book, ask and answer the following three questions:

What do each of your secondary characters want?

How will your secondary characters change and grow?

Which characters will not change by the end of the novel?

To highlight your main character's intense change, it can work well to contrast that person with a secondary character who does not change, and to plan a scene between these two characters near the end of your novel.

I usually develop my characters before I spend too much time on plotting. Authentic, likable characters are important to me, and I don't feel like I'll have the drive to finish several drafts of a book unless I really love my characters.

All the characters in your book should feel like complete human beings, full of complexities. Keep this advice in mind as you brainstorm your characters:

- Make sure each character has multiple layers, not just one, two, or even three. Think of each one like a prism, with multifaceted sides, and keep showing new and fascinating ones to the reader.
- Each character needs something to care about deeply. These needs and desires should be very specific to each character.
- Each character needs understandable motivations. If your character cares about something, chances are your reader will have no problem understanding the reasons for his or her actions.
- Characters should not be fixed in personality or belief. Like people, characters are always open to the possibility of changing. Show characters making choices based on their fears, motivations, and interactions.

Flat and uninteresting secondary characters are almost always a problem in early drafts of books. Always be looking for places you can make characters larger than life. How could they be smarter, funnier, and more talented?

Simple Task: Out of Character

After you've defined the main qualities of your secondary characters, as you did with your main character, figure out what their opposite quality would be. For example, if Sally is generally a very compassionate girl, the opposite of this could be heartless.

Now write a paragraph in which you show Sally acting compassionately, and then another paragraph in which you show her acting heartlessly. What would possibly make her act this way? Exploring another side of her will make her a deeper and more fully realized character and will push you to reach past the obvious when it comes time to draft her story.

Some other opposites could be clean/messy, rich/poor, leader/follower, smart/dumb, quick-tempered/easygoing, and loud/quiet.

In fact, it's a good general exercise to list as many opposite character traits as you can think of. You may not know which character they will work for yet, but having a list to skim may help jump-start the process of getting to know new characters.

Naming Your Characters

Character names are important. Names give the reader an immediate clue about who a character is. Sometimes a name reinforces a character's personality, and sometimes it goes against the grain of a stereotype. For example, I used the name Tessa for the tough, Goth girl in *Losing Faith*, whereas to me Tessa is more commonly used for a subdued or meek character.

If you have already come up with some names for the characters in your story, that's great. But try not to be too terribly attached to them yet. As you explore your characters more deeply in this chapter, you may find good reasons to change some of them.

Choose names that evoke the kind of people that populate your novel. Consider where they live and their ethnicities. Consider whether your characters might give one another nicknames. I like to use baby-naming books to spark ideas, and I often look at the meaning of names to see if they can help me define who my characters are at their deepest levels.

When it comes to finding good names, here are a few hints:

- Don't choose any names you might want to use for your own babies — believe me, you'll tire of them.

- Character names in a novel shouldn't be too similar *or* too varied. If all of your names contain four letters (Mark, Greg, Chris, and so on), they will be easy for the reader to mix up. If every name is unusual or unique, they can also be difficult for the reader to remember or to sound out while reading. Fantasy novels often have this issue.

- Different spellings can change the way you perceive a character. I think of Casey as being a different type of person than a Kasey or a KC.

- Run your character names by your friends. Ask them what type of person they would expect those characters to be, just by their names. It's okay if they peg them wrong, but it's good for you, as the author, to be aware of how others may receive your characters upon first introduction.

- Occasionally, use names that describe characters directly. For example, in a recent book I read, the character named "Tizzy" was, of course, the scatter-brained character and always in a bit of a tizzy.
- Be careful to avoid first-letter repeats, similar-looking names, and rhyming endings. If you're reading a book with a Corey and a Casey, you will likely get those mixed up.
- Want some unusual or evocative names? Check out character names in any Charles Dickens novel. Maybe what your book needs is a Bumble or a Pumblechook!

Simple Task: Name Your Cast

Take the characters you wrote down before, and if you haven't already done so, give each one a name, or perhaps several possible names. Don't forget to list family members and other possible peripheral characters, those who might not appear often or at all but are people your characters might know. If you're unsure what to name certain characters, this is your time to experiment. Jot down possibilities and see how they look on the page together. Add question marks beside the ones you're still hesitant about.

Keeping in mind the list of hints above, how does your name list look? Are any names too similar? Do you want to vary the length of any of the names?

By establishing character names before drafting, you will write faster and help the reader to distinguish and remember characters.

Comparing and Contrasting Characters

The more depth your characters have — each with his or her own motivations and flaws and needs and unique personality — the more complex your plot will feel. Stories with one main good guy and one main bad guy, who compete on a linear journey to see who will win, are ultimately too simplistic. It's the nuances of desire and morality and values that provide your characters with conflict-worthy depth.

Also, not only should each character have variety and depth, but the collection of characters in your story should reflect a similar diversity. This is why secondary characters are as important as your main character, since they will reveal much about your main character.

All characters should interconnect in some way with your main character. To help define them and ensure balance, compare and contrast all your characters. Use the charts I've provided at www.denisejaden.com/fastdraftprintables.html or make your own. In my sample diagram, I've started with my main character in the center. All other characters get listed at the top of the page. I use one chart to mark all the similarities between my main character and other characters in the novel. The other chart notes all the differences.

You can make diagrams for each of your characters showing how they compare with and contrast to everyone else in your novel. Or, make one really big messy diagram, using different colored pens or markers to draw lines between all the character qualities that match up.

Also, each character should represent either an ally who helps or an opponent who opposes your main character's story journey. Write an "A" (for "ally") or an "O" (for "opponent") beside each character's name.

Blank, printable diagrams are available on my website at www.denisejaden.com/fastdraftprintables.html. As a sample, here's a comparison diagram I made for my current work in progress.

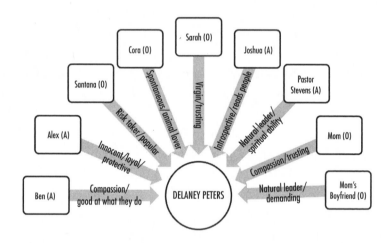

COMPARE

Write the name of main character in circle.

Write other characters' names in rectangles.

Note similarities along gray arrows.

Once you've done this, consider whether every character you've planned for is truly necessary. Are there any characters you can cut? Are there any characters with similar roles who could be combined? Every character should have a clearly defined reason for being in your story. If any characters don't seem to have any commonalities with or contrasts to your main characters, they may be expendable. Or, you might combine a character with a small story purpose with a character with a larger purpose. Perhaps your main character's doctor could also be his uncle, or maybe your main character's best friend is also her sister.

Dialogue

Dialogue is a great tool to further explore and get to know your characters. Dialogue should not be exactly like real life, but it should feel like it could be from real life. Actual conversations include slow pauses, unimportant bits, plenty of hellos and good-byes, small talk, and generally uninteresting banter.

Dialogue should always be smarter, more interesting, wittier, or more powerful than its real-life counterpart.

Great dialogue should work to reveal your characters and their motives without the help of adverbs. For example, you could write: "'Harry, give that to me, please,' he said hurriedly." Or the dialogue could say it all: "Harry, I need that pronto."

Don't be shy about having your characters come right out and say what they think of another character. Characters should say what they want directly, even if it sounds controversial. This approach might cause too much conflict in real life, but it works great in storytelling.

Dialogue should always enhance and reveal the voice of your novel. It should pack a punch.

You can also use repetitive, symbolic dialogue to carry more impact in your story. Sometimes a character will quote a favorite line or phrase, and each usage will have a different impact or meaning depending on the context. In *The Fault in Our Stars* by John Green, the two main characters use the simple word "Okay" to convey a myriad of deep feelings along their character journey. This single word has much more impact than if they'd spelled out their feelings each time.

Is there a word or phrase that might be special to your main character? This does not have to be just one. Brainstorm as many as you like, and see which ones feel right during the drafting phase.

During planning, keep a special section in your notebook for dialogue notes. Often, words and phrases, spurts of dialogue, and first or last lines will come to mind, so jot them down. They may get used during your drafting, or they may serve as inspiration when you get stuck or have trouble remembering your passion for your original idea.

Take Time to Get to Know Your Characters

If you don't take the time to get to know your characters, your readers won't know them, either. As writers, we may assume that we know our characters because we can picture them in our minds, but chances are good that we won't know them well enough to write an engaging and consistent book about them until we've spent many, many hours with them. The following tools can help jump-start that process.

Character Speed Drill

I learned about character speed drills in a writing workshop with Rachel Vail. Here's how it works: Set a timer for five minutes.

Start with your main character and fill in the sentence prompts below with the first thing that comes to your mind concerning this character. Then come back and do the same thing for your antagonist and secondary characters. The more fully you know your characters prior to writing, the easier it will be to follow them through the plot, and the more immediately they will jump off the page for the reader.

I am...
I live with...
My main job is...
I'm really good at...
My mother thinks I...
I hate it when I...
I most admire...
The last time I cried was...
My favorite memory is...
I wish I could be better at...
My dad is...
It makes me really angry when...
The best gift I've ever been given is...
I believe in...
I love it when...
My mother is...
The most embarrassing thing that's ever happened to me
    is...
The thing I want most today is...
My favorite book is...
My dad thinks I...
The best thing I've ever done is...
My favorite thing about myself is...

I feel guilty about...
Three things I can't live without are...
What makes me laugh is...
My favorite movie is...
My biggest secret is...
The worst thing I've ever done is...
What I want most in life is...

Character Interview

I generally complete a full character interview for two or three characters in a novel, and I fill out partial interviews for a few more characters. I find it's always necessary at the very least to do one for my main character. Whenever I get feedback from a critique partner indicating a character feels flat, dull, or cardboard-like, a character sketch or interview is the first place I turn.

Fill in the following for your main character and any other characters you wish (download printable copies online at www .denisejaden.com/fastdraftprintables.html).

The Basics

Full name:
Male or female:
Age:
Education:
Job:
Likes:
Dislikes:
Strong or weak (1–10):
Outgoing or shy (1–10):

Short or tall:
Detailed physical description:

Go a Little Deeper

How does my character feel about him- or herself?
Will this be different at the beginning of my book than at the end?
How does my character feel about his or her father?
His or her mother?
Does my character have any pets?
How does he or she feel about these pets?
What does my character want most in the world?
What does he or she hope to avoid, above all else?
What are five adjectives that would describe my character?
What does my character do with his or her spare time?
Does my character have any hobbies?
Does my character have special talents?
Where does my character fall on the intelligence scale (1–10)?
Where does my character think he or she falls on the intelligence scale?
What was my character's most embarrassing moment?
Proudest moment?
Most hurtful moment?
What is my character's favorite movie?
What's his or her favorite music?
Does my character have any bad habits?
Any habits that annoy others?
Who's his or her best friend?

His or her worst enemy?

What's his or her dream job?

His or her dream vacation?

Ultimately, all of these questions should lead you to answer the most important questions: What is your main character's biggest "want"? And will he or she achieve this want by the end of your story or realize that it doesn't need to be fulfilled?

I know I keep asking this, but it is *important*. Keep returning to it again and again. If the answer changes, compare what you thought before with what you think now.

Simple Task: Character Exploration

Spend five minutes free writing from your main character's point of view. Write about his or her essential "wants" or motivations, or use one of the prompts below:

- The power has just gone out at the worst possible time in your character's life. Why is this the worst possible time? What does your character do?

- Your character looks in the mirror. What does he or she see? What does he or she like or dislike? (The reader doesn't necessarily need to see this, but the author needs to know it.)

- An uninvited guest who will change his or her life shows up at your character's door. Who is it, and what does your character say?

- If your character could go anywhere in the world right now, where would it be and why? Take the character there. Is it what he or she expects?

Chapter Four

THEME

Theme makes books memorable.

What is theme, exactly? When asked to consider the theme of a book, your first reaction may be to cringe, pull away, and run back to your structured plot. This is because many people equate theme with a message or a heavy-handed, preachy undertone.

Don't be afraid of theme. You don't develop your story's theme so you can lecture your readers through heavy exposition. It is for you, the author, to use as a tool as you're writing.

You may never state the theme in your finished book. But knowing the specific themes you are dealing with will give you focus while writing. When your novel gets to a polished state, your themes should be the story's driving force.

Your main themes may not fully emerge until after you've finished your first draft, or even, perhaps, several drafts. And that's okay. Sometimes that's even better. You may go into a first draft thinking you know your theme but come out on the other side realizing the heart of your book is actually a completely different concept. Theme is important because you want your novel to have moral implications, which you can deliver slowly and subtly. This will make your novel more affecting to its readers.

For now, I simply want you to brainstorm thematic words and phrases by creating a "wordle" in this chapter's "Simple Task," below. Eventually, you'll want to condense this visualization into a sentence that describes the main theme of your new novel. Again, this may not happen until after you've written a first draft. When you nail down the exact theme and express it as a sentence, it will likely involve one or more of your brainstormed phrases. Even if this sounds heavy-handed or preachy, that doesn't mean your novel will be preachy. This focus sentence is for *your* use, not the reader's.

A theme describes the moral implications of your story. When brainstorming your theme, therefore, consider the moral arguments and emotional consequences inherent in your story's premise. Once you have a good grasp of these, your thematic moral arguments will seep into the action throughout your entire novel. Your main character, antagonist, and supporting characters will all act out their beliefs on this theme at some point, or at many points, in your story.

Sometimes it's helpful to think of your theme as the setting of your novel. In my debut young adult novel, *Losing Faith*, I considered faith very much a setting, rather than just a theme. Characters worked with it and around it, but faith was always a constant in the background of the novel. Faith is a multifaceted theme, and all the characters in the novel had strong differing opinions on it, so it worked well to keep it as a constant in the background.

Now, let's get a jump on identifying your theme.

Simple Task: Brainstorming Theme

Brainstorm twenty words or phrases that could be used to describe the book you plan to write. Choose descriptive, emotional words that evoke your feelings when you think of your story. Choose words that describe your characters, their attitudes, and how those change. Even if you're struggling with your plot, you can still list the thematic elements that are important to you or that you are passionate about. This may help you launch into further plot ideas.

For example, in my latest novel, *Tent*, some of the thematic words and phrases I've come up with are *miraculous*, *faith*, *danger vs. safety*, *fear of control*, *family fragility*, *true love*, *tough love*, *pride*.

Once you've written down your twenty words, find a visual way to display them. You could scribble them all over a poster board or print them out in different fonts and tape them to your bathroom mirror. You could draw or paste pictures to go with your words. Use any kind of visual display that interests you. The only catch is that you have to be able to leave them somewhere prominent throughout the drafting of your novel.

Here's an example of a visual "wordle" from my work-in-progress novel:

MIRACULOUS **danger vs. safety** **TRUE LOVE** *faith* family fragility PRIDE fear Of Control **TOUGH LOVE**

Remember, this isn't just an exercise for improving as a writer. This is visual inspiration to assist your muse during your Month of Dedication.

Don't leave out this visualization step. Get active with your story. Get visually engaging! Trust me, it makes a difference.

When designing your plot, keep looking at your theme word list. After expressing your twenty words, you may be able to go back to your three-act structure and fill in some of the plot points you are envisioning. Do that now before moving on to the next section.

You will also want to consider how each of your characters feels about the themes you have identified for your story. Look again at your thematic wordle and make notes for each character. If you're tempted to skip over a character because you don't have the answer, this may be a sign that you need to cut that character or combine that role with another character's.

Chapter Five

SETTING

The setting is the time, place, and backdrop in and against which your story takes place. When it comes to settings, I have two criteria: make your settings unique, and make sure they matter.

Your setting should be important to your plot, as this will create a more fully layered story for your reader. Have you chosen a generic "every place" to host your main character's journey? This will give your story a mundane feeling. I recommend spending some time thinking about how you can make your story world unique.

Just as I suggest thinking of your theme as part of the setting, think of your setting as another character in your novel. If you spend as much time making your setting as multilayered and interesting as each of your characters, your readers won't be able to help but enjoy being in your story world.

To begin, picture where you see your characters interacting. Are they in the real world or in an imagined world you will create?

If your story is set in the real world, keep your settings

realistic, but not *exactly* like real life. Exact replicas are boring. Do we need to see every hallway, elevator, or living room your characters walk through? Give us something unique. Real life is full of boring transition moments. Weed out those moments and settings for your reader. If settings such as restaurants, living rooms, generic houses, workplaces, or schools are used, try to imagine unusual or energized versions of these settings.

When it comes to setting, I really look up to fantasy writers. Even though I don't write fantasy, I have learned a lot from their world building and detailed settings. They prove that setting is more than just a generic backdrop against which to place your characters.

In fact, think of your overall story setting like "the arena" in *The Hunger Games*. The coordinators of the games could construct the arena exactly the way they needed each time. You are the coordinator here, and you have the power to shape your world in whatever way you want for maximum dramatic effect. Picture everything that happens within your story as happening within your own imaginary arena. This is where your characters' hopes, desires, needs, and relationships will live or die.

So, pick and choose your settings carefully. If your settings are too varied and spread out, your story could feel fragmented. Don't try to add action or interest by bombarding the reader with new settings for their own sake. This will probably have the opposite effect, leaving the reader feeling confused, distanced, and unable to keep track of the story.

Always look for ways you can tighten the space within which your characters interact. A more compact arena can often lead to more explosive conflict in your story. Keep an eye out for where you can combine your settings (similar to my advice in chapter 3 about combining character roles). Then, make good use of the settings you have. Is there one specific area that your main character could keep returning to throughout your novel? Perhaps your main character's perception of that area could change as he or she changes, so that returning to that area will allow the reader to see that character's growth firsthand.

If your story takes place in a large city or over the scope of an entire continent, consider how you can narrow the scope within which characters interact, to add more potential for conflict. Perhaps you could focus on a certain area within a large city, or maybe a great deal of your action could take place within the airports of a certain continent.

Always ask yourself how you can make the setting more interesting. Even if you're creating a brand-new world, what about this world will interest your reader? If it's a real-world setting, what will make this unique and enticing for your reader?

Then, consider what details of this setting will be important for your reader. Too many details will slow down your story, but not enough may leave readers feeling uninvolved. Of course, even the most unique settings still need to feel like they *could* be real places. They need to feel fully formed, without your giving every boring detail. So, you'll want to sprinkle in telling details throughout, such as during downtimes after high-action sequences. Don't feel you need to describe the entire setting fully in the first chapter. Layering it in will make your readers feel a stronger connection, almost as if they've been there themselves.

A great example of real-world story building is every small-town lawyer story by John Grisham. Readers feel like they have been plunked down right beside the main character in a small-town coffee shop. Every bit of dialogue and every light descriptive passage gives Grisham's settings a realistic yet unique feel.

Making Settings Matter: Building Conflict

Once you have a unique setting in mind, turn your thoughts toward conflict. Settings become like characters when your characters interact with them, as sources of help or as challenges. So consider: What part of your setting might help in your character's journey? What part of your setting might make your character uncomfortable? What in your setting do characters consider important? Are there ways you can increase the opportunity for conflict in the way you build your world? If your setting is a small town, perhaps gossip will play a role, or if it's a big city, might transportation or financial struggles create conflict? Natural environments can be filled with unexpected encounters, and even weather might drive your plot in a new direction.

Consider how your main character feels about his or her setting. Can you think of ways this might change throughout the story as your main character grows and changes? Does he become more ruffled by the small-town gossip, or does she find a new appreciation for the job and city she's a part of?

If your hero has any particular skills, these might lead to unusual settings, or to unusual relationships with your settings. For example, one of my novels revolves around a competitive archer, thus much of the setting revolves around practice and competition locations.

Is there a place of safety for your hero, and what if he or she can't reach it for one reason or another? Is there some place in your setting that your character would fear, and what if he or she had to go there?

On a larger level, consider the mood of your story and how each setting could be used to enhance it. Is the mood dark and ominous or action-packed and alert? Can you make any of your settings more adventurous? Rather than having an average school with an average hallway, might the school have a secret passageway? What if one hallway was rumored to be haunted? Or could you create a school hallway where odd, unexplained smears of blood are found, leading to speculation and intrigue?

Time is another consideration with setting. Over what period does your story take place? Do characters have to meet specific deadlines? If not, can they be made to? The "ticking clock" is a common device used to give a story strong and fast pacing. It gives characters another conflict and something to work against. And it doesn't have to be based on time, just on the threat of some negative action if some other series of actions is not taken. This helps hold the readers' attention and gives them a constant gauge about how much of the story is left.

For example, in the movie *Speed*, Keanu Reeves's character has to keep a bus moving above a certain velocity to avoid the explosion of a bomb. The gas tank becomes the ticking clock. The viewer knows that the gas is going to run out eventually. And just as the audience comes to terms with how difficult this obstacle will be to overcome, the gas tank is accidentally punctured, speeding up the "ticking clock."

Similarly, consider the time period in which your story is set and if there are global or national events that could affect your characters and how they think about the world. What might change if your story took place in New York City just after

9/11, or in New Orleans during Mardi Gras? What about special holidays? If the time span of your novel includes Thanksgiving or Valentine's Day, how will your main character react to that special day?

Logistics and Practical Considerations

Every setting and time period has its own logistics to consider. In particular, technology changes rapidly and may affect your story. Do you have obstacles that require the use of cell phones and computers to help overcome them? Or, conversely, if a simple email would prevent a conflict, how do you avoid it?

How do your characters get around? Does your main character have a reliable car, and therefore getting from place to place will fall into the background? Or might transportation itself become a useful, exciting, and interesting setting, with buses full of odd characters?

If your story is set in a rural or urban area, in a hot southern state or a cold northern one, what are the benefits and drawbacks of each for your particular story? If you can't find specific benefits, perhaps you should choose another setting. These choices *should* affect your plot.

Finally, if you are using a real place to set your story, remember that readers from that area may be more likely to pick up and connect with your book. But it does take a lot of research to get the details accurate.

Before fast-drafting, you don't have to answer all of the questions above. The point is to think of setting as something you can use to add layers to your characters and story. Give yourself freedom when exploring possible settings.

Simple Task: Picture Your World

It's time to create a visual setting for your book. Whether you like to draw, paint, photograph, or clip images from magazines, create or gather at least five visual representations for scenes in your novel. If you want, you can do more than five, since the more you find, the more visually stimulating it will be during your month of drafting.

Using these, make a physical setting diagram, which is a visual clue to your story world. When you are writing, this can help your muse get on board and give you an extra dose of motivation when you need it. You can make this as simple or as complicated as you like. Just make sure it's visual, an at-a-glance guide you can readily understand.

Here's an example of my simple physical setting diagram for *Tent*. It's a compilation of pictures of different settings and

approximately where they will be located within and outside the town where the bulk of the story takes place.

Some writers may want to add roads and maps that will be important to their stories, but in my story, I had three distinct settings I wanted to use, and so I added a few pictures that captured specific scenes I was imagining in those locations. The top left indicates one setting: the tent meetings where many scenes will take place. The middle is the rooted central area of the story: high school. The bottom right is a large church where the climax will take place. Remember: It doesn't matter if anyone else understands your setting diagram, or even knows what the pictures are about. The important thing is that *you* understand it.

Also, your story diagram doesn't have to look like mine. Make it however you wish. Create something visual that you can use to quickly guide your scene setting next month.

Sounds and music are also inspirational and important guides, so I encourage you to make yourself an audio "sound track" or song playlist for your new novel. Your playlist can include as many songs as you like, but I recommend at least five. They don't have to be in any specific order, and they don't have to match your novel's plot in any exact way. If a song gives you a feeling for one of your characters, add it in. Even if there's just one line in a song that makes sense with your story, add it.

Don't skip this step! These visual and audio tools are quick ways to help you battle brain sluggishness or writer's block during your drafting.

Chapter Six

SYMBOLS, IMAGES, AND ICONS

How effective would *The Lord of the Rings* have been if Frodo had been on a journey to destroy a piece of string, or an apple, or a tube of lipstick?

Symbols, images, and icons are important. They can pack so much more punch than a scene full of dialogue or a battle full of action.

Erwin Panofsky was well known for his studies of symbols and iconography in art. His belief was that symbols and icons are understood on three levels. The first level is the most basic: what is the object and its function? The second level links an object to conventional current meanings. And the third level involves intrinsic meaning, historically, personally, religiously, and philosophically.

So, at the first level, make sure any objects you're using symbolically are clearly described so readers can visualize them and understand their function. A reader shouldn't need to be a world-class archer to understand that a character's bow is precious. I must make sure my description of the bow makes the value clear to any reader.

Second, is there a way you can show how various characters perceive each object and its meaning? Does your main character perceive the precious bow as a burden because he doesn't feel qualified to use it, while your antagonist would do anything to get that bow for himself?

Third, how have the objects you're using been perceived throughout history? Have they grown in significance or become more mundane? Are there any philosophical or religious perceptions inherent in your object?

In my novel *Losing Faith*, the very first line starts with an image: "The statue has got to go."

I'm talking about a four-inch Jesus statue, and even though *Losing Faith*'s story is centered around the loss of a girl named Faith, the reader can tell from the opening lines that there is a double meaning at work.

On the surface level, the character is referring to an actual statue. But this statue tells us much about the main character's family and world. What kind of family keeps a Jesus statue on their hearth? What kind of daughter would try to hide the statue?

The theme of faith is involved in much of the story. The statue packs punch to deliver this theme, especially when it shows up again later in the novel.

Symbols, images, and icons are especially effective if you show them more than once, and if they appear in different ways or have different meanings when they show up again. They can be used metaphorically to enhance an idea or to signal a change in ideas or values.

Your images can help you express your theme without being preachy. They are a sneaky, highly concentrated way to get meaning and impact across to your reader.

Look at the thematic wordle you created in chapter 4 (ideally, you've displayed this somewhere). Consider it for a few minutes, and brainstorm ideas for images or symbols that might relate, which you could use throughout your novel. If your story has an academic theme, is there a certain textbook that will mean something significant to your main character? If your story involves a wilderness journey, is there a certain plant with healing properties that will be significant in your story?

Before we go on, spend a minute and think about how you might introduce your symbols, icons, and images. Do you have certain scenes in mind where they will show up? Make notes of those ideas now. It doesn't matter whether you will stick to these ideas or not. Jot them down as part of your brainstorming.

Simple Task: Create Your Image Board

From your brainstormed list of icons, images, and symbols, choose at least five images to visualize and display, just like you did with the physical setting diagram in chapter 5. Either use online clip art, cut out pictures from magazines, or draw the images yourself. This is all preparation to feed your muse during fast-drafting.

Chapter Seven

LIST OF SCENES

At this point, you've done a lot of directed brainstorming about your new novel. Let's pull some of it together and make a list of possible scenes for your book.

Again, there are no rules. This still falls under the category of brainstorming. Don't cross anything out, even if, on second thought, you decide it won't work. All your ideas may be useful in ways you don't expect. Remember, it's not always the ideas that are important. Sometimes it's the *connection* between ideas that you're really looking for.

So, start jotting down any scenes you already have in mind. For each one, try to list the main event of the scene, the function of the scene, possible settings, characters involved, and finally the outcome of that scene.

Don't feel like you have to drum up scenes. Begin with the parts of your story you have already started visualizing. If other scenes don't come to mind right away, put those sections aside and come back to them. Listing your scenes should be an ongoing fun process. Allow yourself breaks so your mind can ruminate.

It might be helpful to think of your last scene first. How will things end for your character? What setting do you visualize for this ending? Where will the final battle or resolution take place? Often it can be helpful to know where your character is headed in order to see the steps he or she must take to get there.

Think of the worst possible scenarios, first for your main character, then for the antagonist and secondary characters. What are they most afraid will happen? Make it happen and see where it leads you.

Look back at the heroic qualities and flaws you came up with for your characters in chapter 3. Brainstorm scenes that will demonstrate those characteristics for your readers. Ideally, you'll want to show the strongest characteristics at least three times.

Do you see a clear beginning for your story? Jot it down. I often have a beginning in mind when drafting, but it ends up changing many times during revisions. So I don't recommend getting too hung up on deciding exactly where to start your story. As long as you start it *somewhere*, that's the important thing for now.

Once you have several scenes written down, consider if you have too many scenes taking place in one setting. I know earlier I suggested combining settings when possible, but you may find as you're listing scenes that you're picturing them all in one place. Can you vary the setting for some scenes?

Also, when mapping out your scenes, consider using jumps in time rather than having transition scenes. Too many scenes in a car or on a plane could be a red flag that you are planning too many transition scenes

You may also have trouble thinking of the outcomes for particular scenes. Don't cut them just yet, but make a note or perhaps put a question mark beside that scene. (I label these scenes with "LP" for "Lacking Purpose.") Not knowing the outcome may indicate that the scene is unnecessary, or it may mean you just don't know the scene's function yet.

Arranging and Evaluating Scenes

At this point, evaluate the scenes you have listed more closely and try lots of new things. Throw your character into different locations with a variety of problems to gauge character reactions or just to see how it feels. You don't have to use every scene you make notes on here. This is an opportunity to be wild with your ideas and let your mind dream big for your characters.

When you have several scenes listed, say ten or more, circle five of your favorites. Take out a blank page, and start to arrange them into a logical order. As you order your scenes, list any gaps between them on your paper, so there's plenty of room to fill in other scenes as you come up with them. I encourage you to pick your favorites because I want you to start with several scenes you're excited about. If other scenes from your original list make sense, add them in. Having this structured on a separate page may help you visualize a clearer story arc. If there are areas that you know will need more scenes, but you just don't know what they are quite yet, circle them for now or highlight them. Don't feel like you need to fill in all the blanks before you start drafting. Sometimes the mind purposely leaves blanks so that your writing has freedom to go in new directions. What you're creating now is just a *basic* framework.

If you get stuck, ask questions like "How will my main character get out of here?" "What if my character tried this?" "How could I make the scene have more consequences?" or "Could I make this problem bigger?"

Eventually, character changes must be shown through action. Can you visualize your main character changing through the scenes you have listed? What situation would make him or her change even more?

Eventually, every scene that's included in your book should read like a ministry. But for now, don't cut any ideas or scenes, no matter how weak they appear. Even those ideas that didn't make your "favorites" list may inspire a new idea during drafting. Instead of cutting the bad, make a note of and highlight your "best" scenes, so you know which ones you will definitely want to write. I'm a fan of highlighting the good with asterisks, bold colors, or pretty little stickers.

If you find it hard to recognize your best scenes, here are some questions to ask:

- Will this scene further the plot?
- Will this scene involve conflict (particularly of morals and values)?
- Will this scene start as late as possible, not needing a lot of setup or background information?
- Does the idea of this scene excite me?
- At the end of the scene, will a character have some sort of revelation?
- Will the end of this scene have power?

Finally, take out a few of your favorite books. Flip through them and look at how the author ended your favorite scenes. Why do these endings work so well?

Endings are often what make scenes memorable and power-ful. Which of your scenes have potential for that kind of power? Star those scenes now, and you'll be ready to move ahead with your story plan.

Chapter Eight

STORY PLAN

Congratulations! Over the past month you've brainstormed all the major aspects of your story. Now I'll help you condense it into a usable story plan for your fast-drafting month. Follow the steps below to formulate your story plan (or download a printable story plan template online at www.denisejaden.com /fastdraftprintables.html). Choose what you would consider your "best" ideas, or the ones that are pulling at you the hardest. Don't throw away the others, as sometimes ideas are deceptively better than they first appear. After completing the story plan, you'll be almost ready to start drafting!

The information you need for this exercise should be included in your notes from chapters 1 through 7. If you haven't come up with any of these details yet, now is the time to brainstorm missing items so you will have a complete story plan all in one place.

1. Start a new page in your notebook, and label it "Story Plan."
2. Write your planned title, or any possible titles.

3. Write your planned drafting start date.

4. Premise: Write your one-sentence story description from chapter 1.

5. Form your three-act structure: For each act, write a one-paragraph description of what will happen in that act (see chapter 2).

6. Write a sentence that describes the main theme of your novel, or list any theme words from the wordle you made in chapter 4.

7. List any important notes on the setting of your novel (see chapter 5).

8. Make a list of your best symbols, images, and icons from chapter 6.

9. Make notes on your characters (see chapter 3):

    A. Main character:

    What does your main character want most?

    What does your main character need?

    What are your main character's heroic qualities?

    What are your main character's biggest flaws?

    B. Antagonist:

    What does your antagonist want most?

    What does your antagonist need?

    What are your antagonist's heroic qualities?

    What are your antagonist's biggest flaws?

    C. Make a list of all your character names for easy reference while you're drafting.

10. Make a list of the planned scenes you came up with in chapter 7. Jot them down in the order you expect them to appear in your novel.

For each scene, list

- the main event
- the function of the scene
- the setting
- the characters who may be involved
- the outcome of that scene

11. Read through your story plan. Are there any other notes you'd like to include? If so, add them.

Now that your story plan is complete, you have an easy reference to return to at any time during your month of fast-drafting.

Chapter Nine

HOW TO WRITE
A FAST DRAFT

By now you should have a basic loose framework of your story. You should have visual clues to your setting and characters. You should have a good idea of your premise and possible themes.

Now, do you want to spend some additional time clipping out pictures of what any of your characters look like, or writing down more details about where scenes will take place? Do you want to visit similar settings around your town to get a feel for them? Go do so.

The goal is to write a 50,000-word novel in thirty days. This breaks down to a little less than 2,000 words per day, but as a round number, strive for 2,000 words. Your main goal each day is to build your momentum and to get your word count down on paper, even if you have to stray from your plan or head in unanticipated directions to do so. If you finish your 50,000-word story early, great! You can stop before thirty days. But I encourage you to read all of part 2's thirty-day plans regardless. The daily prompts may give you added inspiration for or insight into your story.

Most importantly, look at your notes, story plan, and visual displays and know that you're ready.

Say it with me: I'm ready.

Set Your Goal

The one common attribute of high achievers in any area of life — from professional athletes to businesspeople — is that they set goals. Goal setting keeps you motivated, hones your vision, and helps you organize your time.

Fast-drafting sets a specific, measurable goal and includes a clear deadline. I recommend thirty days because it's short enough that it won't interrupt the rest of your life too much, yet long enough to accomplish something notable. I set the daily word goal at 2,000 so your goal is attainable but will still challenge you. It won't take all day, either.

An unchallenging goal may not get completed simply because it doesn't motivate you to get started or to keep with it. You may think, "Oh, I've got lots of time. I can start this next week," or similar procrastination phrases. However, it's proven that a more challenging goal will improve performance.

So to start off, I want you to write your goal down in your own handwriting right now. Set a start date for when you will begin. It could be tomorrow, or it could be a few weeks from now. It could coincide with a calendar month, but it doesn't have to. Then write it down. I mean it. Write it down. It should look something like this:

Beginning on [enter date], I will write approximately 2,000 words per day for thirty days. By [enter date], I will complete an approximately 50,000-word story, and I will [enter what you will do to celebrate].

Write Every Day

This is so important I'll say it again, with extra clarity: write every day for thirty days, regardless of your goals. Even if you don't feel like writing and you're sure that the day's writing time will produce nothing but literary dung, sit down and do it anyway. One key to unlocking your muse and discovering all the creative stories that are inside you is this: momentum.

Momentum doesn't happen on its own, but all it really needs is a tiny push. It takes your opening your document and typing a few words. Suddenly, you'll be typing a few more. Then paragraphs, and then pages. Maybe it will be literary dung, or maybe there'll be a morsel of greatness within your writing that you wouldn't have thought of if you hadn't sat down and let your subconscious take over a portion of the work that day.

Our subconscious won't feed us any good ideas when we're on a writing high and think we already have all the best ideas. Our subconscious mind only kicks in to offer solutions on the days when we're feeling stuck and inadequate and unmotivated.

Also, today's writing may not be awesome, but tomorrow's has a better chance of success if you write today.

Being specific with your goal setting will help with motivation and momentum. You should plan to write 1,800 to 2,200 words a day, or perhaps aim for a weekly goal of 12,500 words, to reach 50,000 words for the month. I suggest 50,000 words because it will give you plenty of first-draft material to work with and a good starting place as you launch into revision.

You might also set a time goal, such as an hour a day, or three half-hour slots, or five fifteen-minute slots — whatever works best for you. If your typing or writing speed is slow, you may need to set additional time aside, but keep in mind that you will get faster as the month progresses. Finally, you created the story plan for a reason, and in part 2, we will use it for inspiration and as a guide to return to when you need it most.

In any case, your main goal is the same: Write every day. No matter what.

Make Your Writing Space Conducive to Productivity

Do you have an ideal creative time? If so, do your best to write during that period as often as you can. If your best creative time is midmorning, but you work or go to school during those hours during the week, make it a priority to block off that time period on weekends. Decide whether early mornings or evenings are a better second choice for work or school days. Whenever you plan to write, scheduling for that time is essential, or else it's likely to get crowded out. Before your month, look at your schedule and figure out when you will write, and for how long, each day. Put this in your day planner with an asterisk or something that marks it as high priority.

Let your family know that this is your writing time and you need to be undisturbed. Prepare some frozen meals ahead if that will free up some writing time for you. Turn on music if it helps you; turn it off if it doesn't. Grab your water or tea or carrot sticks before you start and turn off your phone and the Internet. If these sorts of distractions are a problem for you, look into apps such as Write or Die (writeordie.com), which will add consequences after periods without typing, or Freedom (mac freedom.com), which blocks you from the Internet for a set period. It might only be an hour, but that hour can build an entire novel if you prioritize it.

If it's crowded or noisy at home, consider if a local coffee shop or library will be more conducive for writing. Will you be writing on your commute? Perhaps you'll want to prepare your iPod with some calming music to block out the noise around you. I wrote my first novel at the kitchen table while home-schooling my son. Some people can write just fine with distractions around them, but, honestly, for me it was not ideal. Now I tend to take short snippets of undisturbed time, rather than trying to multitask through an hour of writing.

Find some good places to set up your inspirational visuals for the month. Perhaps you won't be able to write directly next to your visuals, but you can perch them in your bathroom so you'll see them each morning before work. Maybe there's a good spot in your car or dining room for your inspirational visuals. Plan for success and you're much more likely to find it.

Don't Start with a Blank Page; Start with Planning and Passion

One week before your writing month begins, read what you have written in your story plan and in your notebook. Get the creative juices flowing before you start the month. I don't recommend reading your story plan too often during your month of drafting unless you're stuck and you feel like you've forgotten where you're going, or if you're starting to lose passion for your story. The parts of your story plan that feel right for your story will surface on their own from memory, just from your having spent so much time creating it. Always take time to remember what makes you excited and passionate about your story, and write from that place and about those things. The moment you lose interest in what you're writing, your reader will, too.

Each day, encourage and look for new inspiration. In *The Creative Habit*, Twyla Tharp suggests starting a creative session with ten minutes alone simply thinking. Keep your laptop or notebook closed. Engage your mind first. You can think about anything, but my one rule is that you have to think about something you *want* to think about, not something you need to think about. The bills and schedules and commitments and responsibilities can wait. This is time to let your mind wander...perhaps to the hot guy you saw on the bus this morning or the accolades you might receive for doing something great or your last perfect day at the beach. If you don't know what you want or what feels good or what drives you, how will you find these things for your characters?

If your daydreaming inspires you to jump ahead to new places in your story plan, or to write a scene that you hadn't preconceived, feel free to go with it. You have a plan to return to, so you don't have to write your story linearly if bouncing around helps to keep your passion alive.

Daily Tasks and Writing Prompts

In part 2, for every day of your thirty-day fast-drafting month, I provide a "simple task" to help guide your storywriting and inspire you. However, feel free to ignore these tasks if you wish. They are meant to help get and keep you inspired, but don't let them get in the way if you are on a roll. If you're on a certain path that you feel is working, stay with it for as long as it lasts.

That said, I suggest you at least read the tasks each day. You may want to return to some of them later, as all can be used to help you make your novel richer and more layered.

Also, if you complete a task, that writing can be included in your fast-draft word count, but it doesn't mean that what you write must be included in your final manuscript. When it's time to revise, you will shift things around and decide what belongs in the final manuscript and what only serves to help you, the author, know your characters better. The tasks are meant to get your mind-to-finger connection going and to give you forward momentum. Each prompt is designed for a different day of the writing process, but if you're stuck, feel free to jump around. You can always come back to a missed day later, or not at all if you don't need to.

If you feel stuck on a particular day, and that day's task doesn't inspire you, consider using one of the following prompts to get you going:

- Think of what your main character is most afraid of. Make the character face that fear.
- In your last scene, who was causing conflict for your main character? Can you give this opposing character a secret?
- Whatever quality your main character likes best about him- or herself, show the character doubting that quality in today's writing.

Or, if you prefer, here are some writing prompts based on situations or subject matter:

- Take your main character to the beach. What happens and how do others react?
- Show a news report of a shocking world event. What is your main character's reaction? What's the weather like? Add a storm or weather upheaval that changes your main character's plans for the day.

And here are some writing prompts based on sensory reactions:

- In the next scene, have your main character close his or her eyes. What perceptions change? Does the character hear something he or she wouldn't have noticed before?
- Let your main character smell something that triggers a memory. What does your character remember, and why does this smell evoke such a strong memory?
- In the next scene, have your character eat something he or she has never eaten before. Maybe it's gross or scary. Create a strong reason the character never ate it before and an even stronger reason why it must be eaten now.

Writing prompts get your brain working and the connection between your brain and your fingers in motion. Don't stop after a paragraph; keep going and see where it takes you. These exercises help you become a stronger writer.

Always Write Forward

During your thirty days of drafting, don't look back at what you've written over the previous days. By looking back, you'll be tempted to edit, and looking back opens the door for self-doubt to creep in. Each day when you open your document, scroll to the end of what you wrote the previous day and start there. This is probably the most important guideline of this whole book, so I'll say it again:

Don't go over any of your writing until you've written to the end of your story.

As for chapter breaks, it's entirely up to you if you want to plan out ahead of time which scenes will make up which chapters. I don't do this. I like to go by feel. When I sense the start of a new chapter, I simply enter "Chapter ?" and then keep writing. For the first three or four chapter breaks, I can usually keep track of what number I'm on, but eventually I simply insert a question mark. The chapter numbers can be added during revision, and this will help avoid the urge to edit what's already written.

Some of your strongest lines should be your first and last lines of the book as well as the first and last lines of scenes. Don't spend too much time crafting ideal beginnings and endings now. If they come to you, great! The more important thing to focus on during fast-drafting is momentum.

For Accountability and Companionship, Work with a Friend

If you've ever tried writing for NaNoWriMo, or National Novel Writing Month, you already know how much difference a little camaraderie makes. So, if you have a critique partner or just a willing friend, enlist him or her as a helper and cheerleader. Ideally, find someone who will agree to fast-draft with you at the same time. If you have someone you are accountable to, you'll be much more likely to follow through, even on the days you don't feel like it.

Schedule a daily check-in with this person to discuss your accomplished word count. Don't spend too much time talking about the details or direction of your project, as that can give opportunity for self-doubt. Also, you might agree to show or exchange projects on the last day — if not to read, just to prove that you finished. Personally, I wouldn't wish my first drafts on my worst enemy as far as reading material goes, but I would be willing to show someone that I had actually finished.

Twitter is a great way to check in with an accountability friend. That way you can't say too much, but it's a quick and easy way to keep in contact (and others may end up joining you on your accountability journey). I check in regularly on Twitter under the hashtag #wipmadness, and you're welcome to join me there. Come and find an accountability partner if you don't already have one. I also run a yearly challenge with mounds of accountability and encouragement each March on my blog at denisejaden.blogspot.com.

Checkpoints to Aim For

Part 2 guides you in each day of your fast draft. Whether you follow each day exactly as it describes or not, here are the larger checkpoints to keep in mind so that you stay on track. You don't have to write 2,000 words every single day of the month, but strive for it. Meet these checkpoints and you'll have no problem reaching a conclusion by day 30.

Days 1–7: Launching In

Using the daily writing advice, you will introduce your main characters, settings, and obstacles.

By day 3, you should have shown something interesting and/or likable about your main character. He or she should have walked into the inciting incident, or should be close to doing so. Your approximate word count should be nearing 6,000.

Days 8–14: A New Direction

Using the daily writing advice, you will add red herrings and reversals and make new and deeper friendships for your characters.

By day 8, you should be working your way into the second act of your story, where it will take your main character(s) in a new direction or introduce secondary characters and goals. Your approximate word count should be nearing 16,000.

Days 15–22: Deepen the Plot

Using the daily writing advice, you will make your main character's plight worse.

By day 22, your story should be working its way toward the third act and the climax and resolution. Your approximate word count should be crossing the 40,000 mark.

Days 23–30: Race to the Finish

The final week will guide you to a quick-paced conclusion.

Day 30 is just around the corner, and you'll need to look toward a sense of closure for your story. Your word count should be nearing, or above, 50,000 by now, and over the next three days you should complete your story with a satisfying resolution.

A Final Note about Word Counts

If you've done the math, you will have noticed that 2,000 words per day for thirty days adds up to 60,000 words. While I suggest a 2,000-word daily goal, I've set the overall goal at 50,000 words for several reasons. First of all, 2,000 words is easy to calculate and know if you're on track. For example, by day 15, you should have written around 30,000 words. Still, you need some flexibility while fast-drafting. Things may come up that prevent you from writing on a certain day, or that keep you from completing your 2,000-word daily goal. If that happens, don't stress and try to write 4,000 words the next day. The 50,000-word goal provides some leeway here. However, I encourage you to write every single day to keep your momentum going and keep your story in your head, even if you can only squeeze in five minutes before bed.

Don't worry. Stick with me, and I'll help you reach all of these checkpoints!

Now, pull out your written goal. See that start date? Don't let anything interfere with it. Promise me that, at the very least, you will come back and read day 1 on that date.

Stories work their way forward in unique ways. You may not follow all my daily suggestions in part 2, but that's okay. Just like your main character, you need a plan and motivation for your journey. That's what this guide is for.

Onward, Fearless Writers, and I will show you the way...

Part Two

DURING THE DRAFT

LAUNCHING IN

DAY 1

Excuses are the nails used to build a house of failure.

— Don Wilder and Bill Rechin

Have you prepared for day 1 by looking over your story materials from part 1 and getting excited to write? If so, great! Are you feeling passionate about your plot and the new characters you are about to bring to life? Fabulous!

But if this does not describe you, don't worry. If you're anything like me, no matter how much preparation you've done, no matter how jazzed you've been about your story idea and characters, now that it's time to start the actual writing, you may find yourself wanting to procrastinate.

Today, all sorts of distractions could threaten to pull you away from your project. These types of thoughts may enter your head:

"It really wouldn't hurt to start tomorrow."

"But this other thing is *important*."

"I should wait until things in my life slow down a little."

Lies. All of them. And here's why:

"It really wouldn't hurt to start tomorrow."

Why is this a lie? Because it *will* hurt you to start tomorrow. First of all, it will hurt your personal integrity. You've set today as your starting day. Even if no one else has any idea that you skipped a day, *you* will know. And you'll know that you didn't keep your word to yourself.

Also, procrastination only gets easier after the first time. If you put off writing today, then what's another day, and then another?

"But this other thing is *important*."

Okay, that may not be a flat-out lie. Other things in your life *are* important. But the nature of this excuse suggests that your writing goal for the next month is *un*important, which is completely untrue. This is a huge undertaking and one you will be proud to finish. But you can't finish if you don't start. So start.

"I should wait until things in my life slow down a little."

I think we all know why this is a lie. Life doesn't slow down. It gets faster and busier as we age. It gets faster and busier as we accumulate more gadgets, supposedly to improve our productivity. Don't wait. You know who waits to achieve their goals? The people who never achieve them.

Repeat after me: I could wait. Or I could be better than that.

DAY 1 SIMPLE TASK

In terms of story direction, today will be the most intense day because you have to start somewhere, right?

First, look at your physical setting diagram, the picture board you made showing a few interesting novel settings. Pick one to use in your writing today.

Begin with your main character, so your reader knows who this story will be about, and start your story just a little before you think the action really starts. This opening may get repositioned or even cut later, but it will give you a true sense of your main character in his or her "before" state. This is important for you, the author, to imagine in order to make your character and plot authentic.

Right from the start, your main character should want something. This does not have to be the main "want" that will carry him or her through the book. It could be as simple as wanting to get to work on time, or wanting to catch sight of a cute boy in school, or wanting a cup of coffee. But he or she should want *something* that propels the initial action. Give your main character some movement. Don't let the character sit around looking at the scenery. He or she should actively *do* something.

Attempt to write a strong first line that is relevant to your story and its themes, but don't spend too much time on this. Review your thematic wordle, since something might just jump out at you, but first lines often change.

For the first day, think of your main character as if he or she is on a diving board on a hot, sunny day and is preparing to dive in. Over the first few days, your character should, metaphorically, jump off the diving board, going from dry to wet, from hot to sudden, shocking cold. Once the character dives in, everything will change, and he or she cannot go back. This is the inciting incident that propels the character forward. It may take several days to reach this scene, but you should be working toward this big change, the moment of commitment.

The first 2,000 words often feel like the biggest chunk of words during the whole month. If you wish, break it up into two or more writing sessions. Feel free to spend some time exploring your setting and at least one character besides your main character. Today's writing does not have to be perfect. It just has to get done. Like your main character, you are getting ready to dive into your story.

So don't dread it. Enjoy yourself. This is the story that only you can write.

DAY 2

Either life entails courage, or it ceases to be life.

— E. M. Forster

How do you feel when you read a really exceptional book? Does it spur you to write better? Or does it seem to jab at you with the notion that you'll never be that good?

For me, it's a combination of both. Which I feel more depends on whatever else is going on in my life. If I've just gotten a rejection through my agent, or if I've recently received a particularly harsh critique, I'll probably be swayed to feel I'll never write as well. If I've just written a few chapters I'm really happy with, a beautiful, well-written book may inspire me to think I can take those chapters of mine from merely good to actually great.

The thing is, no matter how much we want to write as well as someone else, we can't compare ourselves to others, especially when it comes to writing fiction. Fiction, by its very nature, emerges from who we are at our deepest levels as individuals. Your best will probably look nothing like the best writing by John Green or Ernest Hemingway or J. K. Rowling.

And that's okay. It's more than okay. It's necessary.

To be an exceptional writer, we have to find uniqueness within ourselves. Outside sources can motivate us to look harder within, but ultimately what will make us excellent is mining what is already inside us. Sometimes this is grueling, painful work. It always takes courage because putting your most personal and deepest beliefs into your work, where people can see and criticize them, is scary.

But it's the only way to be exceptional.

So keep reading inspiring work by authors you admire. All the while, remember that they have put themselves out there. Their hearts are on the line in a very delicate way so that you can enjoy their books.

Do you want someone to be that in awe of your writing one day?

Be brave.

Be yourself.

DAY 2 SIMPLE TASK

Today during your writing I'd like you to consider your story's genre.

If you're writing a romance, focus on introducing your reader to the love interest (or at least one of them, if there will be more than one).

If you're writing a thriller, scare the pants off your reader today, even if it's only in some small way.

If you're writing science fiction, show your readers something unique or complicated in this new world that will amaze or intrigue them, so that they walk away trying to wrap their heads around it.

If you're writing a contemporary realistic story, focus on making your story world authentic yet unique. Focus on the atmosphere and mood you want for your book.

Does your story work with a secondary genre? Are there romantic elements? If so, hint at this today. Maybe it's not a standard mystery, but there will be plenty of questions sprinkled throughout that keep the reader turning pages. Focus on those today.

Showing the genre doesn't have to be elaborate or complicated. Find out what your story is and show that on the page today in your own unique way.

DAY 3

It's like driving a car at night. You never see further than your head-lights, but you can make the whole trip that way.

— E. L. Doctorow

You know who impresses me the most among fast-drafters? The unpublished. It's true, and you know why? I remember what it was like before I had anything published because it wasn't all that long ago. I remember what it was like before my family and friends took my writing seriously. I remember how difficult it was to stand up not only to everyone around me but to my own niggling self-doubt.

All writers, published and not, live with high amounts of self-doubt, but I admit it can be easier once you've had some publishing success. It may not help fend off your own insecurities, but it can help others take you and your writing goals more seriously.

The first year I attempted to write a novel in a month, I remember, I was frustrated with everyone in my life on a daily basis. I was yet-to-be-published, and many people in my life thought of my writing as nothing more than a time-sucking hobby. They often confronted me about how I was making their lives harder with my month-long writing goal.

This added lots of conflict and stress to my life. Relationships suffered. I became angry and bitter. Here I was, attempting something so incredibly difficult, verging on impossible, and no one was helping me with it! In fact, they were fighting me!

Fast forward a few years. Now, I have published books, and people see my writing as something more than a time-sucking hobby. But, to be honest, the biggest change is not in the attitudes of others but in my preparation to handle my writing challenge.

Each year I've been getting better at preparing for my month of writing by thinking of how I can best fit my goal into *everyone else's* lives. You see, I've noticed that I write better when I'm under less relational stress. So I do what I can. I mentioned some of these things in chapter 9, but they bear repeating, now that you're immersed in your fast draft. Try getting up half an hour before the rest of the household to write so it doesn't interrupt anyone, or stay up half an hour after everyone else has gone to bed. If you haven't already done so, spend one afternoon preparing some frozen meals for dinner over the next week. Don't get discouraged by your typing or writing speed in the first few days — it will get faster as the month progresses.

I realize now that, in the beginning, I was saying to my friends, in effect, "Stop EVERYTHING! I have to write." Now I've claimed it as my own personal goal that I'm going to make work, even if it means a few sacrifices. Most of them are only personal sacrifices. Now my actions say, "As you were. Nothing here to see." And in fact, since then, my husband has completely forgotten about my writing goals during several month-long writing jaunts.

All it takes is a little preparation to bring some added peace to your writing life.

DAY 3 SIMPLE TASK

On day 3, I've asked you to focus on others, and I'd like you to consider having your main character do the same thing. How can your hero act selflessly to help someone else?

This task is part of creating likable characters. It's important to establish their likability early on, even if the main character is initially making some mistakes or poor choices.

If it doesn't make sense for your main character to act self-lessly in today's writing, can you insert this in the form of a flashback, or have a secondary character or your love interest act selflessly? Blake Snyder wrote a wonderful book on screen-writing called *Save the Cat!* The premise, quite simply, is that the simple act of a character saving a cat will make him or her likable and a character readers will want to follow.

Here are a few suggestions to jump-start your creativity:

- Have your character save a hurt animal.
- Have your character skip a meal or miss out on sleep to help someone.
- Have your character miss a final exam in order to help someone else.
- Have your character use hard-earned savings to buy groceries for someone in need.

All of the above examples involve some sort of self-sacrifice. Even if it's a small sacrifice, this can embody your character's larger selflessness in an endearing way.

There's a reason that adding a selfless act works so well in fiction. We are surrounded by *selfish* acts every day. Think of the last time you went grocery shopping. Was the parking lot crawling with people just waiting to offer you the next parking spot? The last time you were at Starbucks, did the folks already in line offer you the space in front of them?

Selfless people are uncommon; that may be one of the rea-sons we look up to them. If the selfless act you add doesn't work, you can always take it out during revisions, but I encourage you to try adding a selfless gesture for your main character. It may even help you like the character more yourself.

Today's writing should also involve one of the images from your image board of symbols and icons (from chapter 6). Choose one and think of it as you're writing.

This prompt doesn't have to be difficult or worked in perfectly. Let your main character play with an object. Just let her hold it, move it, or look at it. Something subtle. The object can grow in significance later in the novel, or you may realize later that there's a better object to open your book with. For now, use it as a placeholder that you can always come back to and change.

As I described earlier, in my novel *Losing Faith*, I mention a Jesus statue in the first line and a few times in the first scene; its early significance is to show the main character's embarrassment with her religious family and her antireligious plans for the evening. But the statue grows in significance in later scenes. In early drafts, I had tried other objects in the same place instead, such as a Bible and a condom wrapper. Sometimes you have to play with a few images to find out which one works best with your theme. But that's okay. Fast-drafting is for playing.

Go and play. Learn something new about your characters today.

DAY 4

My mom was a phoenix who always expected to rise again from the ashes of her latest disaster. And in spite of her self-doubts, she had a very strong sense of who she was. She had a sense of self-worth. She loved being Judy Garland.

— Lorna Luft

This process takes a lot of faith. Faith that fast-drafting will actually help you. Faith in the storytelling process and that a germ of an idea can actually grow into a fully realized novel within a month. Faith in your characters and that they will be interesting enough to carry your story.

But most of all, faith in yourself.

Your faith will be tested. Maybe not today, and maybe not next week, but chances are good that it will happen during your thirty-day journey. I'm telling you this now so you won't be surprised or feel alone in it. There's a reason they call it a leap of faith and not a step of faith.

The thing about faith is this: overcoming a crisis can make you much, much stronger.

For instance, imagine this scenario: A religious woman loses her husband of many years, who dies an unexpected early death, leaving her without companionship or someone to pay the bills. At that point, she may question her faith, asking, "God, are you real? Are you a good God, like I've always believed? Or are you just an idea that sounds good when everything is going well?"

As you can imagine, the woman enters a very dark season. Not only has she lost her closest human companion, but she's now lost her beliefs. Or has she? The thing about faith is, all it takes is a tiny seed to come back and grow with a vengeance. That's faith at work.

Three years later, if we check in with this woman, will we find that the seed of faith remains dormant? Will she still be living in a state of anger or bitterness, feeling like she's misplaced her life's hope?

Or will the seed of faith have grown and become much stronger than it ever was before? If this woman survives her dark season, and comes to know and be comforted by her God in the face of adversity, she won't be as fragile if another huge tragedy hits her life. It likely won't rock her faith a second time, or at least not to the same degree. Her faith is strong. She is strong.

So I encourage you, when your faith is tested in your story or yourself, hold fast. You will have dark moments of doubt during this month-long journey, but hang on and preserve a seed of hope and you'll be fine. That seed will grow much quicker and stronger the second time around, after you've faced some adversity.

If you come away from this month with a completed manuscript, that is something to be proud of. But if you come away with a renewed and stronger faith in the process and in yourself? That will serve you for all your days to come.

DAY 4 SIMPLE TASK

Today, return to your main character's goals. What is his or her main need or desire for this journey? Review your story plan to refresh your memory. Have you shown the reader this need or desire yet? If not, show it today.

Does your character have the faith he or she needs to succeed? Does he or she have a seed of faith? Show us that seed in some small way.

Why is your main character's desire important, not just to the character, but to all of us? He or she should want something that we can relate to, and today I want you to identify what that is. Universalize that desire. Have someone else in your story relate to it, either in the same way, slightly differently, or in a completely different way so your main character initially can't see the similarities.

In this way, you show the reader why he or she should care, too, or why anyone or all of us should care.

If you have already shown the reader the main need or desire, spend today making that need deeper. Perhaps a small bit of backstory will help the reader understand why the character needs this so badly. You're nearly 8,000 words into your story now, so a little backstory in small doses will not hurt. Hopefully your reader is now committed to walking the journey along with your main character and will be happy to learn more about him or her.

Today is also a good day to add a bigger question for the reader. You may have already been dropping small questions to keep the reader turning the pages. Today, let the reader really question a character's motives, even if those motives won't be explained for some time yet. Or put your main character in a situation that will be seemingly impossible to get out of gracefully.

Your reader will enjoy spending time considering the possibilities and solutions.

DAY 5

The best thing about writing fiction is that moment where the story catches fire and comes to life on the page, and suddenly it all makes sense and you know what it's about and why you're doing it and what these people are saying and doing, and you get to feel like both the creator and the audience. Everything is suddenly both obvious and surprising ("but of course that's why he was doing that, and that means that...") and it's magic and wonderful and strange.

— Neil Gaiman

Visually restimulate your inspiration.

Think of the book you're working on as a movie. Let's pretend it's a year down the road, and your book is finished and polished and on its way to becoming a bestseller. The people from Paramount have contacted your agent and are interested in optioning the film rights, but they'd like your input first.

We're just dreaming today. Obviously. Go with it.

The first question they ask is: "Who do you think should play the main character in the movie?" (Because, you know, big-time producers always want an author's input about this sort of thing.) "Do you have any suggestions for the antagonist, and the secondary roles and bit players?"

The producers love your feedback and keep asking for your advice. "Where do you think the movie should be filmed? What city, town, or neighborhood would suit it best? What's the color palette? What can you hear as the sound track? Are there particular songs that fit certain scenes? Are there special effects?"

This exercise isn't about evaluating whether your book has potential as a movie. This exercise is meant to get you visualizing your world and the people in it. Before writing today, see and hear and experience some of your story as if you were watching it as a movie. Play a few inspirational songs from the playlist you created during your planning month. Plus, it's just plain fun.

DAY 5 SIMPLE TASK

If you're looking for some new inspiration, take your movie visualization and apply it to a new scene: How would these actors, this setting, and this sound track unfold? What if Zac Efron played the love interest for your next romantic scene? What if Ellen Degeneres was the wacky aunt at the family dinner table during one of your confrontations?

Write that today. Don't worry if it takes you out of the progression of the story. Allow yourself to play a little, and perhaps the scene will get shifted somewhere else on a later draft. Just have fun today to get your creative juices and excitement for this story going.

DAY 6

Serious writers write, inspired or not. Over time they discover that routine is a better friend than inspiration.

— Ralph Keyes

There is no such thing as "waiting for inspiration." It's an oxymoron. Inspiration doesn't come through the waiting process. It comes through the *doing* process. All your best ideas are going to come out of the process itself, not from a bolt of lightning or a muse-struck moment while you're meditating.

Remember when you were brainstorming for this draft? What were your biggest eureka moments during your brainstorming? Were they well-thought-out ideas that had been brewing in you for years? Or did they seemingly just appear one day out of thin air? Did they come when you were staring at a piece of art on your living room wall, or when you were on the elliptical machine at your gym?

Perhaps it wasn't even an idea that was the big *aha*, but just a connection between ideas. This is the process of doing in order to bring inspiration.

It is a known fact that, just as a watched phone never rings, your muse won't appear while you're staring paralyzed at your work in progress. Muses are sneaky. They like to sidle up beside you when you're busy with other thoughts. They like to pretend they've been there the whole time.

How many people have you met who seem to have a great idea for a book (or they *think* they have a great idea for a book)? Almost every person I meet, writer or not, likes to tell me about his or her Great Book Idea.

The difference between them and you? You're actually writing yours. You're not waiting for the day when the kids are grown or you cut back your hours at work or the story is fully formed from beginning to end in your mind. You're not waiting for inspiration to hit you like a tsunami so you can stay up for three days straight and write until your fingers bleed.

You're doing it here and now. In thirty days, no less. And you're doing it regardless of how you feel.

DAY 6 SIMPLE TASK

Today I'd like you to focus on showing your main character's biggest weakness. All great characters need flaws, and your main character is no different. Look back at your story plan if you need a reminder. Then, take a moment and reflect on your own personal flaws. How do your personal flaws affect the way you've been living your life? How do your character's flaws affect the way he or she is living life?

Flaws often cause wounds. Who is your main character hurting, simply by virtue of this flaw? If your main character is hurting someone in your novel, this can cause a great moral dilemma for your reader. Of course, your reader wants to root for your main character. But what if that means watching that character hurt another? Whose side will the reader be on?

Adding this sort of moral dilemma may feel scary. What if you lose your reader's allegiance along the way? What if your character cannot be redeemed in your reader's eyes?

But a deep moral dilemma will make your reader care more. It'll make you dig deeper to find unique and powerful ways to redeem your main character. No one wants to read about the perfect character, a do-gooder, going through life helping everybody. Bor-ing!

Your readers will pick up your book because it offers plenty for them to think about. It'll make them rethink their alliances and their core values.

So make the flaws big and bad today. Don't be afraid of them. They'll make your writing stronger for the rest of the month to come!

DAY 7

You get lazy, you get sad. Start givin' up. Plain and simple.

— James Dashner, author of *The Maze Runner*

What if you knew it would work out?

When I began trying to get published, I admit, I thought it would be easy. I thought my first manuscript was pretty engrossing, and at least as good as the latest *New York Times* bestseller I had read. I was certain I'd have my pick of agents and editors clamoring to pay me millions of dollars.

I don't think you'll be shocked to hear it didn't work out that way. It was, in fact, my third manuscript that ended up getting me representation from a smart and savvy agent and, eventually, a sale to a wonderful publisher. But I have to tell you, as time went on and I submitted manuscript after manuscript, building a pile of rejections taller than my car, I definitely started to doubt success.

In the midst of this, though, I realized something about the books I was reading. They all had one thing in common: a confident use of words. And I started to wonder if my lack of confidence was leaking into my writing voice. Was my writing actually getting worse as I was losing hope in my ability to get published?

This revelation caused me to forcibly stir up hope in myself. Quite honestly, I don't know that I even believed my hopeful words to myself at first, but I continued to say them to myself anyway. Each day when I sat down to write, I repeated to myself the same mantra: This will be the one. This will be the manuscript that sells.

And you know what? It helped. It must have, because that manuscript really was the first one that sold.

If someone came along and assured you that this book you're working on now would get published, impact throngs of people, become a bestseller, and [insert personal goal here], would you write differently?

What if you *knew* you would succeed?

Write that way, live that way, and you will!

DAY 7 SIMPLE TASK

Today is a day for action, both for yourself and for your characters.

I'll bet you've got some great tension going on between some of your characters by now. With the addition of selfless acts and flaws and objects and goals, chances are your characters are becoming increasingly interesting and layered.

Ideally, if you haven't written about it yet, you have already been thinking of your inciting incident. These smaller tensions your character has been feeling should be leading to a greater conflict, something that will happen or, better yet, something the character *makes* happen that will forever change his or her life.

Today, aim to hit that moment.

If you've already passed your inciting incident, concentrate on making a character do something that will raise another question. Perhaps a secondary character gives away a secret that makes the reader wonder if he or she is trustworthy. Or perhaps the love interest does something that indicates that one of his or her major goals is in conflict with your main character's goals. The reader will wonder how this can possibly be reconciled.

These are the types of questions you want to feed your reader, and yourself, so you'll keep writing to find the answers.

A NEW DIRECTION

DAY 8

Good is the enemy of great.

— Jim Collins

Why are competitive athletes so inspirational to the rest of us? Because they're beyond dedicated. They train hard, often while the rest of us are still sleeping. How many days do you think a competitive athlete wakes up in the morning and thinks, "Ugh, I don't feel like giving everything I've got today?" How many days do you think he or she does it anyway?

So here's my advice to you today: do it anyway.

Maybe you woke up this morning with your brain swarming with new ideas that will make your novel into the perfect literary masterpiece. Maybe all that creative energy is bursting forth and carrying you to your computer, where it will rush out of your fingertips and onto your keyboard.

Or maybe it's going to be work today.

Four out of the five days per week that I go to the gym, I don't feel like going. I don't feel like I have it in me to give it all I've got, or even a little bit of what I've got. But I've made myself a deal: If I can get myself to the gym on a day I don't feel like it, I can warm up on the exercise bike and read a chapter of a good book. If I don't feel like working out after that, I give myself permission to go home without a workout. You know how many times I've gone home without a workout?

Zero.

Right now, make a deal with yourself that you'll open your document and *start* every day. You'll write for ten minutes as a warm-up, and if you need it, give yourself a reward for the warm-up alone. Reevaluate after you've done ten minutes of writing. Could you do a little more? Would you feel more satisfied and prouder of yourself if you pushed yourself a little further?

Reading makes an excellent secondary warm-up. Keep a few inspirational novels that you love right beside your desk. Allow yourself to read a page for every two that you write. Don't just read to get swept up in the story, but read to notice what sweeps you up. What draws you in? What doesn't? Don't worry that the author's work will seep into your story. On days when you need a push, it's about doing the work and "training hard." Your story will remain *your* story. Sometimes you just need an inspirational shove from a professional trainer to get going.

DAY 8 SIMPLE TASK

By the end of day 8, your word count should be around 15,000 to 16,000. If it's lower, I encourage you to try to write a little more today. Try to sneak in an extra writing session, or have a word-count race with your accountability partner.

Day 8 is also a good time to evaluate if you're ready to launch into act II of your story. Consider:

- Have you introduced your major characters and their main needs and detailed something likable or interesting about them that will keep the reader reading?
- Has your inciting incident occurred?
- Is your main conflict under way?

If the answer to any of these is no, focus on getting those things instigated or completed today. At this point, you should be completing act I so that you can start act II.

If you have accomplished all of the above, then you are entering the middle of your story's roller coaster. For the next two weeks, you will focus on character development and those unexpected twists and turns that knock your main characters off course. If you're in the flow of this, keep going. If you need some added inspiration, review your story plan and consider what events you've already anticipated, and then consider how they fit with any new events that have come to you while drafting act I.

First, to start act II, your main character should be seen reacting in some strong way to the inciting incident. How he or she reacts will be a strong indicator of what is to come through the rest of the story. Write this today if you haven't already.

Then take the story in a different direction.

Is there another love interest (or a love triangle) you can introduce?

If you're writing a mystery, or a novel with a mysterious

subplot, can you introduce a red herring and take your main character off in the wrong direction?

Can you introduce a new obstacle for your main character?

Can your main character get distracted by a new character or a new goal?

This is the time to be moving in new directions, whether those you've preplanned or ideas that have recently come to you. If you don't know exactly where you're going, take a step anyway and see where it takes you.

DAY 9

Nothing in the world can take the place of persistence. Talent will not; nothing is more common than unsuccessful men with talent. Genius will not; unrewarded genius is almost a proverb. Education will not; the world is full of educated derelicts. Persistence and determination alone are omnipotent. The slogan "press on" has solved and always will solve the problems of the human race.

— Calvin Coolidge

It's easy to tell stories. We do it every day. "Did you hear about what happened at the club last night?" "Guess what happened to my boyfriend on the bus this morning?" "I have to tell you about this movie I saw last night."

We're natural storytellers at heart. You've likely been telling stories your whole life. But all this time, you haven't doubted your stories. In conversation, we just tell it like it is, or like we remember it. We don't spend time thinking about the correct words to use to tell the story about this morning's bus ride. We don't put that much pressure on ourselves.

Why do we do that with our novels?

When you listen to others talking, what makes you want to listen to their stories? Is it their word choice? Their evocative details? More likely, it's simply their exuberance for their story or their confidence and comfortableness as storytellers.

Write your story as it naturally wants to come out of you, even if it will later take some elbow grease to jiggle the plot into a working machine. Let your own unique voice and excitement show through. Don't spend time thinking about how to tell it, or if you're telling it as someone else could tell it. Tell it like you told a story at the party last week or by the coffeepot at work the other day.

Don't overthink. Just write.

DAY 9 SIMPLE TASK

As we're launching into act II, today I'd like you to think about subplots. Are some of your secondary characters' stories becoming more obvious as you're writing? Have you shown their goals and desires, and are some of them contrary to your main character's goals and desires?

Are any characters hanging out on the periphery of your story, but you just know there is more to them?

Show us more of one of your secondary characters today. Make the character's story real for the reader; make the case for what the character wants. Perhaps this desire can lead to a whole new set of complications. If so, great! You have yourself a subplot. If not, don't worry. You're still learning a lot about your characters, how they need, love, and even hate one another.

DAY 10

Everything yields to diligence.

—— John Marks Templeton and James Ellison

How's your writing energy? If you're anything like me, by day 10 it starts to taper off. You've been writing some pretty big chunks of story for nine days straight, after all.

How do you regain lost energy? I can suggest a few ways.

1. Know what's zapping your energy. Chances are, it's not your story. Do you have more on your plate this week at work or at home? Are things starting to pile up? Are you finding yourself putting things off that you know you should do, and the procrastination is weighing on you? Maybe it's time to reevaluate your schedule or ask for a little help. Make clear choices about what you need to do and what you don't need to do, then don't feel guilty about the things you put off. After all, writing a novel in a month is a *big* goal. But it is only one month. Some things can wait.

2. Stop talking yourself down and complaining. My son has certain chores he has to complete each week, including vacuuming the upstairs rooms and cleaning the bathrooms. Some weeks he spends at least twice as much time complaining about the chores as he actually spends doing them. By the time he gets around to doing the work, he's exhausted. I can see it all over him. Whenever he has a better attitude and does his work without complaint, I always ask him how hard he thought it was. His answer: "Pretty easy, actually."

This applies to writing, too. If you spend your time scrutinizing your writing and thinking it's no good, that you can't do this, and that your book is going downhill, guess what will happen? It'll zap all your writing energy. Or if you spend your time complaining, to yourself or others, about how difficult it is to write every day, guess what? It will be.

3. Are the people around you adding to your energy or taking away from it? I have certain people I purposely avoid when drafting a new novel, especially highly critical and negative people. On the flip side, I have a dance teacher who is very motivated; he is constantly creating new dances and improving his skills. I also have superdedicated writer friends with stellar attitudes. These are the people I try to spend my time with during a month of fast-drafting.

4. Get some exercise. It sounds contrary to your purposes, doesn't it? If you don't have the time and energy to write, how on earth will you drum up the time and energy to exercise? But trust me, energy evokes energy. A person who spends regular time going for walks or working out at the gym generally has more energy than the slothful person who camps in front of the TV all day. Today, spend the first fifteen minutes of your writing session going for a walk. You might find the effort has a bonus: movement can get your creative juices flowing. Perhaps you'll work out a story idea along with working out your body!

DAY 10 SIMPLE TASK

Today, focus on highlighting a symbol, icon, or image. Either introduce a new one or reintroduce one that the reader has already seen. Look at your image board. What could you work into your story at this point? Or can you come up with something brand new?

Also, raise another question for your reader today. This could be about your main character or about the secondary character you were working with yesterday. Remember, questions keep the pages turning...

DAY 11

I am a great believer in luck. The harder I work, the more of it I seem to have.

— Coleman Cox

Why do we want what we want? Why do we want to be published, bestselling authors? Or why do we want to have beautiful, silky hair and rock-hard abs?

We have a dream. Inside our heads, we surmise that things will be better, easier, more enjoyable, or more exciting if we achieve our dream. Sometimes we let ourselves fantasize about unrealistic dreams because we desperately want more from our lives. Our characters do this, too.

Other people's opinions matter. We often want to pretend they don't matter as much as they do, but it's likely that most of the things we do in a day are motivated in some way by what someone else will think of us.

Sometimes we fantasize that accomplishing certain milestones will make us care less about people's opinions and become more secure in ourselves, but that often is not the case. When it comes to their bodies, bodybuilders and fitness competitors are some of the most insecure people I've met. Published authors often doubt their writing ability more than unpublished writers.

Take a minute and imagine: What would you wish for if a genie appeared before you right now offering three wishes. Now consider *why* those are your wishes. Play them out in your mind. What do you think would change if you attained the things you are wishing for?

Oftentimes in books and movies, when a character makes

an over-the-top wish and it is actually granted, it does not work out how the character expects. Does that represent something accurate about dreams and personal satisfaction?

What would your main character's three wishes be? If they were granted, would it change his or her life in ways the character expects? If not, then how?

Knowing ourselves more thoroughly helps us know our characters. Take a few minutes today and think about *your* dreams and desires.

DAY 11 SIMPLE TASK

Today, as your main character meets obstacles and reversals in act II, focus on the character's dreams. Let your character fantasize, perhaps in a short dream sequence, about attaining his or her ultimate dream. How realistic are the character's expectations. Would things change the way he or she expects?

A different approach would be to bring on a terrible occurrence that is out of your main character's control. However, the character's dream could be what gives him or her the focus and strength to do something about it. This helps to show your character's mettle.

Dreams and wishes, even if unrealistic, are opportunities to show a character's inner strengths and flaws.

DAY 12

With ordinary talent and extraordinary perseverance, all things are attainable.

—— Thomas Fowell Buxton, 1st Baronet

Comparison is a project killer.

During the days when I was first pursuing publication, I swear, it seemed like every other writer I knew was getting a book deal. Not only that, but I'd swap work with critique partners, and it seemed like every writer I knew, published or not, was so much more talented than I was.

I spent hundreds of hours scrutinizing and comparing my work. I compared it to my critique partners' and to every book I read. If not for some wonderfully encouraging people, I'm sure I would have given up the pursuit of publication.

We don't always see ourselves clearly, and we don't always see our creative ventures clearly, either. The truth is, when it comes to creativity, comparisons are fruitless; it is apples to oranges. No two stories are the same. No two voices or vocabularies or novel structures are the same.

Despite realizing this, I was still convinced that once I was published, I would stop comparing myself and my writing to others. Believe it or not, after I was first published, the comparisons actually became *worse*.

First, I compared book deals — how many books were contracts for, how big an advance, what about foreign rights and movie deals (or the lack thereof)? Comparisons were constantly in the forefront of my mind. Who made the bestseller lists and got awards and reviews — the list went on and on. Since I only had a one-book deal and I wouldn't hear from my editor for three months at a time…it must mean I wasn't a worthy writer. My publication was probably a fluke.

If you're spending *any* of your time comparing your writing or career to others', I encourage you to nip that in the bud. It is a time and confidence suck, and it will only grow and grow, no matter what your accomplishments.

The next time you are tempted to compare your work to others', stop. Someone will always seem better, and someone will always seem worse. Comparison is a slippery slope that will not help you get your manuscript written or published.

DAY 12 SIMPLE TASK

Who does your main character compare him- or herself to? Do these comparisons make the character feel better or worse? In what ways are these comparisons revealing? Today, show your character reflecting on and comparing him- or herself to other characters in your story. Take a moment to glance over your character compare-and-contrast diagrams from chapter 3 for ideas.

You might compare your character in a way that shows your main character bringing renewed focus to his or her goal. A nice act II twist is for that goal to seem closer than the character thought, which provides a false sense of security about reaching this goal.

This false sense of security will allow your character to relax — possibly too much!

DAY 13

I think a hero is an ordinary individual who finds the strength to persevere and endure in spite of overwhelming obstacles.

— Christopher Reeve

If you're anything like me, from time to time you get disappointed by the whole writing and publishing biz. Not only that, but the truth is, you probably have a right to feel down in the dumps.

Today, I just want to encourage you not to stay there. It doesn't matter how much *right* you have to be upset, or how wronged you have been, or how overlooked your writing has been. Let's call this state of being exactly what it is: self-pity.

And who does self-pity hurt? Certainly not the publisher or agent or writing partner who has wronged you! Self-pity holds only one person in bondage, and that's the person who nurtures it.

I have writing friends who garnered hundreds of rejections before that same book went on to become a bestseller. I also have writing friends who have gotten such positive feedback they were sure a book deal would follow, and it threw them into months of nonwriting despair when it didn't. I've heard from writers whose book contracts were canceled after months of hard editing because of changes in publishing personnel or in the market.

Things happen. In the business of publishing, many of those things are completely out of our control. Don't let those things dampen your winner's attitude because, trust me, anyone who can write a novel in a month must have a winner's attitude. Today, let go of self-pity. Anything that holds you in a pattern of negative thinking about yourself or your work...release it. Hold up your chin. Decide not to let the words or actions of others affect your efforts.

Take charge of your own emotions concerning your creative ventures!

DAY 13 SIMPLE TASK

If you followed yesterday's task to show your main character comparing him- or herself to others, today calls for a reversal. If your character thought he was better than someone yesterday, show him today in a worse light. Alternatively, if your character thought she was lacking compared to someone else in her life, today show her trumping this other person.

If your character felt a false sense of security yesterday, pull the carpet out from under him or her. Make the character realize he or she blew it, or at the least have the character see that the main goal is much farther away than he or she realized. Break your main character's heart a little, and the reader's heart in the process. Set the stage so your character must take a risk to get what he or she wants.

If yesterday's comparisons led your main character to feel doubt and wallow in self-pity, show the uselessness of that reaction. Make the character see that self-pity and comparisons do not lead anywhere. Show the character's newfound awareness of what he or she needs to do to reach the goal.

DAY 14

I — think — I — can — I — think — I — can.

— from *The Little Engine That Could* by Watty Piper

Mantras work.

Remember *The Little Engine That Could*? How did he make it over the hill? By positive affirmation. It's true. There is power in our words and in our thoughts, especially concerning ourselves and our abilities. As you believe, and as you speak, so you will be.

So watch what you say to yourself. Does your self-talk sound like this: "I suck." "There's no way I'm going to get through this." "Who is ever going to want to read this pile of worthless chicken scratch?"

Or is your self-talk more like this: "I think I can, I think I can." "This is a gem in the rough. It just needs to be polished." "I am writing toward victory." "I'm not alone with a blank page. Not anymore." "I'm on my way to success." "I'm a do-er, not a watcher."

Choose whatever positive affirmation or reinforcement you want. What do you want to be better at? Recognize your small accomplishments in those areas. If you'd like to be better at organizing your time, for example, say, "I'm learning to make my writing and myself a priority. The organization will fall into place." If you're struggling with your self-esteem as a writer, focus on your diligence and how that will breed skill.

Remember that the little blue engine in the story really didn't know if he would make it over the hill. It took everything in him to say the words and to believe them. At some point, we all get hit with discouragement that feels impossible to overcome. Face that discouragement. Find and use a positive mantra in those moments. This is what will make your stories memorable, that perseverance.

It's what makes us champions.

DAY 14 SIMPLE TASK

By the middle of act II, let self-doubt trouble your main character, so that the character considers changing his or her goal — temporarily. The recent shocks and reversals perhaps bring on a loss of faith, a sense that meeting the bigger goal is too much to handle. Or maybe he or she is nearing the crest of another hill and becomes too tired to continue.

It's too early to make your main character a champion. Let doubt take the character down a notch, so the reader sees how hard the journey is. In this discouraged moment, have the character decide to pursue a different, easier goal, perhaps in the belief that it's more appropriate. Switching to a lesser goal is not something anyone does without regret. Let your reader feel the character's regret, but have the character make the decision anyway.

Your main character will not remain focused on this new goal for too long, however, as circumstances will soon make clear that this is the "wrong" goal. Soon after this, let the character start yearning inwardly for the original goal again.

Also, just as you've done for yourself, pay attention to your character's self-talk. It will likely sound defeated as goals change, but it should shift as that direction is rejected. Let the self-talk reflect this shift, and devise a line that he or she will say more than once throughout the story.

DEEPEN THE PLOT

DAY 15

And where I excel is ridiculous, sickening work ethic. You know, while the other guy's sleeping? I'm working.

— Will Smith

It's day 15, and you're halfway through your fast-drafting month. How are you doing?

Today, spend a few minutes taking stock of where you're at with your word-count goal. You committed to writing 50,000 words in thirty days. If you've followed my suggested goal of 2,000 words per day, then by the end of today, your word count should be around 30,000. However, if it's at least 25,000, then you're right on track.

If so, wonderful! I encourage you to treat yourself to a piece of chocolate cake after today's writing. If your word count is less, and particularly if it's hovering below 20,000, consider what's been keeping you from achieving a higher word count.

Are you struggling to make your daily writing a priority?

Do you feel the goal was too lofty or that you're writing too slowly?

Whatever the case, strategize how you can overcome these problems over the next 15 days.

It's important to fix whatever the problem is so that you are making a genuine effort to reach your goal. You see, it's not just about this goal. In general, people who achieve goals are more likely to achieve future goals. On the flip side, those who fail at their goals, don't write them down, or don't follow through, are also more likely to fail on future goals. This is the case with any goal — not just writing goals. So, in a way, what I'm saying is... finishing this book could also help you lose weight and earn more money!

So, treat the next fifteen days as if there were life-and-death consequences to finishing your book. No matter how far along you are, I'll bet you can do it. The first step is to clarify your new daily word-count goal: take the number of words left to write and divide it by fifteen. Then, draft a new handwritten goal, such as this: I will write 2,685 words per day for the next fifteen days.

Post this statement where you will see it daily for the rest of the month. Sign it and date it. The process of writing out a goal helps to solidify it and make it real.

Remember, lose weight, make more money, and... finish a book!

DAY 15 SIMPLE TASK

Today is a great day to bring one of your images back to life in your story.

Can the iconic green Mustang that's always made your hero cool get into an accident that renders it worthless?

Could your main character find something precious in the garbage?

Consider what images you have used so far in your novel and try to come up with the most shocking or devastating thing that could happen to one of those items.

How will showing this icon again affect the way your character is thinking about his or her goals?

DAY 16

Art is eternal, for it reveals the inner landscape, which is the soul of man.

— Martha Graham

Are you getting bored by your story? Come on, be honest. It happens to all of us. It happens to me. Often.

Sometimes along the path of writing we forget what's important in our story. What first sparked your interest about writing this story? Can you remember? There must have been a moment when you thought, "Yes! This is going to make an awesome book!" What, specifically, sparked that feeling? Was it a certain character or a certain plot point that you thought was fresh and new and would take readers by surprise? Was it an emotion you could relate to strongly in your characters?

If you find yourself getting bored with your story, you may have strayed away from that initial spark during writing. Perhaps you first thought this story would really affect people, but now that you're into the nitty-gritty of it, you wonder if it's worth all this time and effort.

It is. Trust me. If you're having trouble telling yourself that, let me be the one to tell you today.

No one sees the world in the same way you do. That's why it's important for *you* to tell *your* story. It could be that you have been spending too much time comparing your story (a first draft, no less) to other books you've read. Or perhaps you have been too focused on reconciling plot points and forgetting the story aspects that fell into place seamlessly. Your mind is in fast-drafting mode right now, and you're not seeing the full picture well enough to judge it. It's still the same brilliant idea you had a month ago, and a month after you finish writing this draft, you'll be able to see that again. Have faith in the process.

Where's the story that only you can write? It's the one that captures your experiences and emotions and love for your specific characters. Focus on that, and you'll be back on track and excited about your story again before you know it!

DAY 16 SIMPLE TASK

Without rereading, what's your favorite part of your novel so far? If you had to pick a favorite scene, which one pops up in your memory? Can you re-create what worked in that scene in today's writing? If you're bored and have lost that spark, write in whatever way, or about whatever character, inspired your original passion. Even if this scene doesn't "fit" with the story plan you developed, take this detour to respark your interest. This may be the direction the story needs to go, anyway.

If you're not struggling for enthusiasm, focus today on bringing your antagonist around in full force. A sudden attack by the antagonist will make your main character realize who he or she really is and the importance of the original goal. This will cement the character's need and desire and give another flash of your character's strength for both you and the reader.

DAY 17

If you can find a path with no obstacles, it probably doesn't lead anywhere.

— Frank A. Clark

Sometimes looking back at a string of daily writing bursts can play tricks on your mind. You began with a vision for this book. Do you find that, despite your focus on that vision, maybe it's getting hazier?

This can happen when you're in the thick of a project. You focus so much on that initial visionary burst of creativity that "today" doesn't measure up. Or, you spend so much time trying to work out individual plot points that it seems like it'll never come together. Instead, take some time to think of your successes and find reassurance. While writing this book (and during other writing efforts) you have certainly had plenty of good, and even some great, writing days.

Not every day is like that. They won't be. If there were no valleys, you wouldn't be able to recognize the mountaintops! If the middle of this month has seemed filled with valley days, chances are, your mind is just overlooking the good days. Try not to focus on the down days, since you can't do anything to fix the days that have passed.

Instead, close your eyes for just a moment and think of the end of this book. Think how good it will feel to type "The End." Think about persevering, and know you will have more of those wonderful bursts of creativity if you do.

Then focus on today, just today. Don't let yourself dwell on any problems you are trying to work your way out of; just take one more step closer to that ending. Don't worry about tomorrow or the direction your story is taking. Just think about today, about this chunk of 2,000 words. If this thing you're making is enduring growing pains, that's a *good* sign. It means your baby is truly growing to completion!

DAY 17 SIMPLE TASK

Answer one of the questions you've laid out earlier in the novel in a surprising way for the main character today. Perhaps the character reacts differently now compared to during a similar situation earlier, and in a way that shows a budding new strength.

Is your main character having growing pains as well? Let him experience one of those occasional, exciting bursts of excellence. Show the character's special brand of smarts or skill in some strong way. Is she an athlete? Have her beat her own record. Is he an engineer? Have him solve the problem no one else could solve in a way that shows the extent of his knowledge. Have your character enjoy the fruits of this success today and worry about tomorrow when it arrives. It's good advice for all of us.

DAY 18

It was a high counsel that I once heard given to a young person,
"Always do what you are afraid to do."

— Ralph Waldo Emerson

Do you throw your entire self into your writing, heart and gut-wrenching soul, or do you hold back, unsure of how your whole self will be received? Have you been settling for mediocrity?

Expect more of yourself.

Here's the question for today: what do you think dreams are made of?

Do you think that some authors put in half effort and by some stroke of good luck their books become bestsellers? Do you think that bestselling authors have a special gene that makes them *feel* like sitting down to write each day?

Don't be discouraged by someone else's success or by someone's failure to help you along your way. There is room for your success in this world, and no one can stop it but you. Your perseverance and hope are what will ultimately help you reach your goals, not what others do for you. Your destiny is not tied to anybody's actions but your own.

I know what you're thinking. "But if the editor/agent/publisher/reader doesn't give my book a chance..." True, you can't control editors and agents, and they have bad days like anyone else. The day they read your manuscript may not be a good day. However, whether fair or not, rejection comes with the territory.

This makes hope and perseverance even more vital! The writers who decide it'll never happen for them, they'll never get their break and realize their dreams; they are ensuring that they won't.

But you can control your destiny.

Who do we admire? The people whose lives seem to fall together perfectly for them? Or the people who never give up hope and push through toward their goals, no matter the circumstances?

Start with controlling your pesky emotions rather than letting them control you. Don't allow a bad attitude to keep you from a day of writing. Don't give in to the feeling that you just don't have it in you to crank out even a single word today. Don't let your emotions have control.

I recently read Joel Osteen's book *Every Day a Friday*. The premise is basically that it's proven that people are happier on Fridays. Is this the effect of the moon on the tides? Or do people decide to be happier because they're looking forward to a weekend?

Emotions *are* under your control. You can choose to be happy and motivated and hopeful.

Take control of your book and your life. Decide right now that this book will get written. You'll realize your dream, and you don't need to count on any other person, or even being in a good mood, to do it!

DAY 18 SIMPLE TASK

Yesterday you worked at showing your main character's special skill or smarts. Today, possibly using your own frustration to fuel you, show your character's frustration. Even though your character is skilled, talented, and smart, it's not enough. Show the reader this desperation.

To make things even worse, find someone in your story who can break your main character's trust today. How will your character react when these things are heaped on altogether? As you near the end of act II, you want to continually raise the stakes.

DAY 19

If you're going through hell, keep going.

— Winston Churchill

Your main character's lowest point is coming. This moment is what some screenwriting teachers call the "dark night of the soul."

What makes us cheer for our favorite characters in our favorite novels? We see them at their lowest points and then we see them *overcome*. There's no real victory in an easy journey. What if all Frodo had to do in *The Lord of the Rings* to destroy the ring and bring peace to the land was hand it to the local blacksmith in the next town? Would we have cared?

His journey and goals were very nearly insurmountable. We can't imagine withstanding what he withstood, and that's what makes us admire him and want to continue reading.

If there's struggle, then success becomes something to be proud of. And it's something others will be proud of, amazed by, and in awe of.

Have you had a personal "dark night of the soul"? My dark night was in 2011. Over about four months, I had a painful and devastating miscarriage, my dad died in a sudden and shocking work accident, my son gashed his head open and had to be rushed to the hospital, and my husband's place of business burned down. I'm proud to say that I overcame the shock and heartache and pain and fear and confusion of that time, and I think I'm a better person for it. What's interesting now is watching the reactions of people when I tell them about my experiences in 2011. With the first tragedy, they tilt their heads. By the second one, they're shaking their heads. By the third and fourth, their eyes widen in disbelief and awe.

We have to be willing to push our characters to these places that will make people's eyes widen — to present seemingly insurmountable, overwhelming challenges that our characters have no choice but to face. To do that, we have to mine our own past experiences.

What was the darkest night for you? And how did you come out on the other side?

DAY 19 SIMPLE TASK

Start bringing your main character toward his or her dark night. Take things even farther than yesterday's broken trust. Can you reveal more to make it a full-blown betrayal? Perhaps not just one character but someone else very close to your main character was in on the betrayal.

Or perhaps something your character has hoped for from the beginning of the novel is put completely out of reach today. A character expecting a promotion actually gets fired. Or a character counting on a marriage proposal gets dumped instead. Make the damage seemingly irreparable.

From this point on, you want to keep making things worse and worse for your main character — so much so that you'll brush the line of believability. Your readers' eyes will widen, and that's exactly what you want.

DAY 20

Do not follow where the path may lead. Go instead where there is no path and leave a trail.

— Ralph Waldo Emerson

A dream starts in a tiny little unseen place within. When it starts it's only a speck of a seed, and by nature, we seem to know this seed is a fragile thing. We keep our dreams to ourselves at first. And that's good. It's maybe even necessary for a seed of a dream to survive.

A transition follows, and I think this may be where people lose hold of their dreams. When your dream moves from an inner place to an outer place, it risks many things. It can be drowned out by criticism. It can become anticlimactic if it doesn't provide what we were hoping for.

Chances are, some if not most of the people in your life are aware of your fast-drafting goals this month and of your writing goals overall. You've been writing furiously every day (or nearly so), and they see your focus and dedication. Some will be genuinely supportive of your goals. Some will have high expectations for you and your month-long project. Others might not. In the guise of offering all sorts of well-meaning advice and "words of wisdom," they may actually be questioning your efforts, talents, or purpose. Or maybe they simply want you to stop so life can return to normal. If this is the case, and you're losing motivation, take action. That poor little seed of a dream is in danger!

Spend some time and water your seed with inspiration daily. Seek out those people who truly support you. Remember the moment that first sparked your story idea. Go back to that feeling and pour it over your dream like water. Fan your hopes and expectations, and find a safe place to nurture them that's protected from the "elements" of doubt and criticism. Only you can keep your dream strong and alive.

Ideally, by fast-drafting, you will strengthen your writing dream this month, making it more likely to survive no matter what terrain it gets scattered on. But around midmonth, it may still feel tiny, so do everything you can to protect it.

Also, don't just share your goal. Share your dream, your hopes and expectations for your writing, with others. If others know how much you care, they are more likely to support you. It's as if you're passing them the watering can. However, voicing your dreams creates its own strength. Even if others continue to stand around and scrutinize your garden, criticizing your efforts, it will have less effect on you. You will be too busy tending to the little seed of your dream.

In fact, when someone asks you how your writing is going, avoid the temptation to complain. Don't focus on the pitfalls and struggles, or that you nearly threw your laptop across the room this morning. Be positive and focus on the big picture. Tell them you're nearing the end, and you're really proud of many of the things you have written this month. Because that's the truth, isn't it?

Everything, including creativity, needs the right conditions to thrive and grow. Give your dreams everything they need.

DAY 20 SIMPLE TASK

As you're keeping your dream alive, focus today on whatever is threatening to kill your main character's dream. Show your character's growing strength and maturity through how he handles these attacks, but allow the dream to come very close to getting completely snuffed out.

The "dark night" or lowest point is still coming for your main character, but show the reader small glimpses of strength — which will foreshadow the eventual victory!

DAY 21

Most people never run far enough on their first wind to find out they've got a second. Give your dreams all you've got and you'll be amazed at the energy that comes out of you.

— William James

As a writer, especially of long works like novels, you may find it a daunting task to stay motivated all the way through until the end. What if you reach day 21 and suddenly realize there's a major kink with your main plot arc? Or that your main character has a major unlikable flaw, but he or she needs it in order for the plot to work?

At this point, it's quite possible these kinds of thoughts are starting to plague you. You're far enough along to realize any mistakes you've made, and you're thinking ahead to the next draft. You're realizing what a huge revision this story is going to need, and you might be wondering how on earth you're going to drum up the motivation for the next draft when you haven't even finished the first draft.

That's the problem. There's absolutely no way to drum up enough motivation for two drafts at once. So don't try. Don't contemplate the next draft, or it will threaten to zap all your energy for this one.

At this point, you have only one goal: to get to the end of your 50,000-word first draft. Your job isn't to fix all the problems or to make it a page-turning bestseller. Maybe you were hoping you could do both during your first draft. If so, lay some mental groundwork for the revisions that are ahead of you, but the truth is, while you're fast-drafting, you have very little perspective on what your book will need. Right now, stay microfocused on the scenes you are writing. While any larger plot or character flaws may seem huge and unfixable, there's a pretty good chance that they're not. You started from a strong story plan, after all. Even if you've strayed from that plan, and your detour hasn't panned out the way you anticipated, it will be easier than you think to pull it back toward a strong workable route in revisions. You'll need perspective to know for sure, and that's hard to get in first-draft mode, when all the writing is close-up, like looking at your story through a magnifying glass.

As you fast-draft, give yourself and your manuscript the benefit of the doubt. Make each scene as good as you can make it while you finish the draft. Feel free to tweak things as you go to improve any flaws you're starting to see. Make notes for later revisions if you like, but then put those notes out of sight. You don't have to come up with solutions until you've shelved your completed manuscript and put it out of your mind for a while. Only then are you likely to come up with the *best* solutions.

For some people, the urge to revise may seem like a pretty, yummy candy dangling in front of you, enticing you, but it'll leave you empty, irritable, and unsatisfied — just like real candy. Finish your draft. Typing "The End" is what will leave you the most satisfied. I promise.

DAY 21 SIMPLE TASK

Maybe your main character has also been too caught up looking off into the future. Perhaps the character is depressed or frustrated over losing hope. Instead of dwelling on this, have the character become microfocused and concerned only with today, with right now and what the character can do in this moment to change his or her life.

Let the little bit of confidence your main character gained yesterday — whether from newfound calmness, brilliance, or maturity — propel the character forward. With this confidence, the character will make a new, better plan for how to achieve the main goal. This plan, he or she believes, is so much better. Let the character spend time working it out and corralling "the troops" to help bring this plan to fruition.

By putting his or her whole heart and soul into this plan, your character will be devastated when it doesn't work out, and this will help lead to the "darkest" night possible.

DAY 22

Effort is only effort when it begins to hurt.

— José Ortega y Gassett

The Shiny New Thing. If you're anything like me, a shiny new story idea will be hitting you any day now. You'll compare it to the one you're writing, and it will probably outshine it in more ways than you can count. You may think about it day and night. You'll wonder, "Maybe I could write half of this one by the end of the month instead! Would it hurt to put this first draft aside to explore this other shinier idea that I'm so excited about?"

Yes. Yes, it would hurt.

Every single story idea is fraught with problems and complications of its own. Even though it *seems* shiny and exciting and downright brilliant, this new idea is only truly one thing: fresh. You haven't spent days and weeks thinking of all the possible problems. You haven't tired of characters or relationships or plot points. Of course it *seems* better!

If your attention starts to wander to other ideas, renew your excitement about this current project. In fact, if it has lost your excitement, then do something exciting with it. Insert an unexpected major conflict. Maybe somebody really important needs to die. Maybe some character reveals a huge secret that even you didn't realize.

Sometimes, as we write step-by-step through a novel, we take a step that leads the story in an unproductive, unmotivated direction. No need to go back and read to find it. You'll know. A little birdie on your shoulder will remind you.

If your passion is no longer on the page, think back to the

last plot point that made your emotions swirl. Don't go back and change everything. That's for the next draft. Just go back to that exciting place, emotionally, and use it as inspiration as you write forward in a different way. In a way that excites you.

Excitement will always make for better writing. It will give you added confidence, which will automatically make your writing stronger.

And be sure to call this Shiny New Thing exactly what it is: distraction. It won't get you to your goal. You're so close now, and you've already dealt with so many other distractions. Renew your passion for this story, and it'll be no problem to get back on task to reach toward the finish line.

DAY 22 SIMPLE TASK

While you're giving up on your shiny new idea, your main character will be getting attached to his or hers. Remember the plan the character came up with yesterday? With this new plan in mind, take your main character into "training mode." How can the character make him- or herself better, smarter, stronger in order to carry out the new plan? Is there a new ally who can help the character train harder than ever before?

This training will set your character up for a hard fall tomorrow, when the "dark night" arrives, but unbeknownst to your character, it will also help him or her achieve eventual victory.

RACE TO THE FINISH

DAY 23

Things are never so bad they can't be made worse.

— Humphrey Bogart in *The African Queen*

Writer's block? No problem. Let me help you with that.

I give you permission to write complete and utter garbage today. There, I've just freed you from the debilitating problem of writer's block. You see, writer's block really isn't about being *unable* to write. Did your fingers just fall off? Are you unable to type on the computer? No, and even if your fingers did fall off, you could just download a program or phone app that records speech. Lost your voice, too? Oh well, better give up.

Writer's block is fear over not writing well. Or not writing well enough.

And some days, I guarantee, especially while fast-drafting, you won't feel like you're writing well. So let's just get that unasked question out of the way up front. Are there days I don't feel like my writing is good enough? You betcha! It's true for every single writer who ever put pen to paper. But you have to write anyway. Write garbage. Write something that you'll come back to in a month and a half and laugh at because it's so bad. Write something that you'll be able to show your fans when you're famous so they can laugh, too. Write something that will give depressed writers a surge of hope, so they will exclaim: "Wow, if they wrote *that* and still went on to write wonderful books, maybe there's hope for me, too!"

Push through today, and then see what happens tomorrow. I predict that suddenly "writer's block" will have disappeared and is no longer a problem for you.

Or, just focus on volume. What's your word count, by the way?

By day 22, you should have written between 37,500 and 44,000 words. If you're in this range, simply maintain your current pace and concentrate on wrapping up your story the best way you know how. You'll probably write more than 50,000 words, but that will just be more fodder for you to work with during revisions.

If, however, you're lagging behind the 37,000-word mark, I encourage you to take out your calculator again and figure out what daily word count you need to aim for over your last eight days of writing. Write that number down and stick it on your bathroom mirror or steering wheel. Sprint to the finish and reach 50,000 words. While the number itself is not essential, it's important to bear down and conclude your character's journey, so you have a complete story to work with on your next draft.

DAY 23 SIMPLE TASK

During today's simple task, all of your main character's planning and training is for nought. Or at least it seems that way. He or she has given this plan absolutely everything. Today, make something drastic happen to thwart the plan. Maybe someone has to die today, or maybe the death will only be metaphorical. Your character's hope dies. This is the dark night of the soul that you've been working toward, when everything looks as bad as it's ever been. As you're writing, keep asking yourself, "Is there any way it could get worse?"

After the dark night of the soul, when your character is in despair, start thinking about the climax of your novel. Tomorrow you will be launching into act III, and there will be a drastic turnaround for your character. Think about what will bring the change — what will spur him or her on again. Then think of how you can make this climax bigger, stronger, and more extreme for your main character. Have you planned a showdown between your main character and the antagonist? Where could you set this showdown that would make it even more exciting and fraught with conflict? A good approach is to set your climax in a very confined space, which will add to the tension of the moment. By the end of writing your character's dark night of the soul, perhaps you could have brought your character here, and the location will play into your character's renewed motivation.

DAY 24

*My philosophy is that it's better to explore life and make mistakes
than to play it safe and not to explore at all.*

— Sophia Loren

Are you a risk taker? I admit, I'm not. Not usually, anyway. My
husband has always been the fearless one — the type of person who trusts that the rent money will appear from somewhere
by the end of the month, who will blurt controversial comments to crowds of people and worry about the consequences
later.

I'm the type who balances my checkbook carefully and
thinks long and hard before I speak, in fear that my words could
be taken the wrong way.

But there is a saying: Nothing risked, nothing gained.
There's some truth to that.

When I look at my life, there's one area where I'm not completely risk averse. I've taken up writing and transformed it from
a hobby into my profession. I've sent many a manuscript to the
big scary New York publishing houses and elsewhere around
the globe. Those ventures are not for the faint of heart.

But I've had to discover the risk taker within me, the side
that is dying to try more. The side that will push fear aside,
no matter the risks, and attempt things I've only dreamed of.
Then again, the nice part about writing is that there *is* still a
safety net.

Until I show someone, it's all just words on the page. No
one has to see it if I don't want them to. All it takes to get rid of
the very risky thing I've done and the consequences that might

follow is to hit the delete key on my laptop. Or drag the embarrassing file to the trash icon on my computer. Or save the writing in a new file marked "This Didn't Work."

Take some risks in your novel today. Go in dangerous directions, even if they may not work. Push your characters farther than you think they would normally go and see what happens. Make sure this book will be exciting for *you* as well as your reader.

If you take off on a tangent that doesn't work, don't worry about it. You can retrace your steps back to the highway. You can go back and fix problem areas during revision; not now, but later. Now is the time for taking chances, trying new things, finding out how far you can stretch your characters and what they are really made of. Don't be afraid of having fun or putting your characters in pain. It will get you to the depth of your story faster than anything else.

DAY 24 SIMPLE TASK

If you're writing into the climax and it's going well, keep with it.

If you're having trouble pulling your main character out of his or her dark night of the soul, chances are it's because things are not bad enough. Things need to get so bad for your character that he or she *has to* change, *has to* dig and mine his or her inner resources for the strength to move out of the dark night.

At this point in the story, you can't get too extreme. If your main character is not on the verge of death, take things farther.

Look at your main character's need. Is it really a need, or up to this point, has it only been a desire? How can you make your character's need for this greater?

Keep pushing today to find out what your main character is made of.

You're into act III now, and from this point forward, you will want things to move even more swiftly toward the final conflict, without any detours or false climaxes.

Which other characters might add to the tension if they appeared during the climax? Perhaps a parent or a friend who might take the opponent's side, or a teacher or a boss who shows up at the worst possible moment.

As your main character is getting stronger and stronger, look for ways you can make the situation worse and worse.

DAY 25

There is nothing to writing. All you do is sit down at a typewriter and open a vein.

— Red Smith

Unfinished novels have one thing that finished novels do not: promise.

Some writers will find themselves self-sabotaging at this point because they don't want to lose that promise. After you finish, you will have to take stock of what you've done and how well you've fulfilled that promise, and you may fear the result is not as stellar as you had hoped in the beginning.

Rest assured: Upon finishing your fast draft, you will not be asked to take stock. In fact, this is the *worst* time to take stock, since you need some chill time to be able to shift from micro-mode to big-picture mode. Upon finishing, you will be asked to bask in rewards and congratulate yourself for your persever-ance. You will have finished, after all!

And here's even better news: What you finished is only a *first* draft. Your manuscript still has lots and lots of promise and potential. If you were expecting to write a masterpiece on the fly, simply adjust your perspective and expectations now.

I know I've said that you should always be working forward and not looking back, but today, if you like, read the first couple of pages from the first few days of fast-drafting. Don't read any-thing recent, and nothing more than the first couple of chapters. Resist the urge to edit.

Looking at those pages, ask yourself a few questions:

1. Is it better or worse than you expected? I'll bet it's better, and I suspect there are good lines in there that you don't even remember writing. Chances are, there are segments like that throughout the whole draft.

2. What promises do you think these pages make to the reader? Have you fulfilled those promises? (If not, don't worry — there's still time!)

3. What remains to finish the story arc your main character initially began? Does a naive character still need to become knowledgeable and worldly? Does a character with a chip on his or her shoulder still need to shake it off?

These are just questions to ponder as you focus on how to resolve the main story conflict and tie up all the major loose ends. Perhaps you can't wrap up everything neatly, but for the final scenes, shift your perspective so that each scene engages the book's overall journey.

DAY 25 SIMPLE TASK

With your main character's overall story arc in mind, focus on the flaws that have surfaced over the course of the novel and make them integral to the unfolding of the climax. The climax is a great place to have your character recognize this fatal flaw, perhaps for the first time, and to see clearly how this one personality trait has been a drawback that's undermined or impeded his or her entire life.

By focusing on this weakness, you also keep the reader in suspense about whether or not this character will truly overcome the antagonist, even though he or she has already pushed through the dark night and desperately wants to overcome. Even let the character appear to be defeated, only to discover victory at the last possible second. Overcoming the opponent should be the most difficult thing the character has ever done.

DAY 26

Go to the edge of the cliff and jump off. Build your wings on the way down.

—— Ray Bradbury

As you tie up the climax, you'll spend the final fast-drafting days focusing on what your character has learned on his or her journey. Now I'd like you to take a moment and think of all *you* have learned about writing and about humanity over the past month. That, my friends, is what the journey of writing fiction is about. If *you* come out ahead in knowledge and wisdom and understanding, isn't that already success?

Now, focus on your readers. Let's help them come out ahead from the experience of reading your book, too. Self-revelation should be hitting everyone at this point: your characters, your readers, and you.

Your characters should be more aware, like looking into a mirror and finally seeing one's true self. This self-awareness, more than any other thing, is what will transform your main character into a hero.

This moment of honest evaluation should be one of the most difficult moments for your main character. Self-revelation never comes easily. It always takes courage. Your character has been holding those truths at bay, refusing to see them for his or her entire life.

DAY 26 SIMPLE TASK

At this point, you should be answering some of the big questions of your story. During these last few days, you should continually take stock of where you're at in terms of finishing act III and your entire draft.

Have you found the lowest point for your main character, which takes superhuman drive to pull out of? Have you had a moment when it seems like your main character's opponent will surely win? Has your antagonist revealed his or her strategy? Has your main character clearly overcome his or her opponent?

If so, then focus on making your main character's self-revelation evident. How can your main character recognize the core of who he or she is, or who he or she has become through this journey? Will another character call it out? Will it come in a private moment of self-revelation?

If you haven't answered these questions, the next few days are your chance to hit these things hard!

DAY 27

Never confuse a single defeat with a final defeat.

— F. Scott Fitzgerald

There are critics everywhere: in your home, at your workplace or school, probably even among your writer friends.

You can't avoid criticism, and the worst criticism of all is self-criticism. It can stifle you into literary silence, and it's probably one of the only things that can stop your momentum at this point. The difference between someone who can finish a thirty-day writing challenge and someone who cannot is in his or her ability to silence critics.

If you're not willing to take chances, you won't be able to maintain your creativity. If you keep listening to critics, fear of failure can be paralyzing.

Have you struggled with self-doubt? Great! Welcome to the club (it's a really large club, by the way…every writer I've ever met is a member). But you can't live in self-doubt or under criticism while you're trying to be creative. You just can't. It may seem impossible — you may have received three rejections this week, or maybe your closest critique partner just said your latest project is worthless — but you need to step past the self-doubt. You need to remember that everyone goes through this. Stephen King received hundreds of rejections before he was published. How much self-doubt do you think he experienced? What if he'd just given up or let his self-doubt taint his writing?

We've all been through this. So put any doubts out of your mind and push through anyway. You're almost there!

DAY 27 SIMPLE TASK

By now you should be finishing the climax and working toward the resolution of your novel.

As you do, consider the following questions:

Does the resolution maintain some momentum? Seek a balance, so that the very end is not too slow and drawn out, or such a whirlwind that it leaves your reader confused and needing to reread what just happened to figure out what's going on. My early drafts always tend toward the whirlwind side of things, so now I purposely focus on expanding details and scene setting during and just after the climax. Even if you can't fix everything at this point, keep this in mind for later revisions: you may want to resolve some plot points earlier, so you don't have so many details to tie up during the last chapters, and during the climax, you may need to expand on the setting, action, and emotions.

Also, make sure your main character has clearly reached his or her goal or else found and achieved a more appropriate outcome. Did the original goal give the character everything he or she needs, did he or she find an alternative, more satisfying outcome, or did the character find that what was needed was within all along?

In the resolution, also focus on how relationships have been taken to a new level, been changed by new revelations, or been left behind.

DAY 28

Perseverance is the hard work you do after you get tired of doing the hard work you already did.

— Newt Gingrich

A lot of people decide to watch a movie rather than working on writing a tough scene.

A lot of people don't make it to the gym on a regular basis.

A lot of people frequent McDonald's.

What do all of these people have in common? They take the easy way out.

You, my friend, have not taken the easy way out. You're almost there. Now cross that finish line, even if you have to crawl!

Pareto's 80/20 rule originated as an economic formula, but many motivational speakers have expanded it to this thought: 80 percent of the people are only going to get 20 percent of the results they want, and the remaining 20 percent of people are going to get 80 percent of the results they want.

Many writers start a draft of a manuscript and never finish it. During National Novel Writing Month in 2011, there were 256,618 participants and only 36,846 writers who succeeded in finishing a 50,000-word novel. That's about a 15 percent success rate. The rate of success during NaNoWriMo is similar each year, and I suspect many of the same people cross the finish line year after year.

By reaching the end (you're almost there!), you're counting yourself among the small percentage who have succeeded — and who will succeed time and time again.

DAY 28 SIMPLE TASK

Look at your wordle of theme words, and consider the following questions:

Is your main character's story arc evident?

Is your theme evident?

Can you make either of these more obvious by showing them or having a character voice them?

At the end, you want everything about the outcome and themes of your novel to be crystal clear. So I encourage you to focus on clarifying themes and expressing them in as many ways as possible at this point. During revisions, you can always back off and make them more subtle, if necessary.

DAY 29

Easy reading is damn hard writing.

— Nathaniel Hawthorne

You're so close you can taste it!

These last couple of days might still be difficult, especially if you have too much story to tie up in two days. But I encourage you to wrap things up anyway. Write to *an* end, even if it's not *the* end that will finish the book in later drafts. Get an ending on paper, even if it's not told the way you had hoped. Then, once you get some distance (and possibly some other opinions), you can evaluate one way or the other how the book works as a whole.

When I drafted my second young adult novel, *Never Enough*, the original ending took my main character, Loann, off to college and back home again, fast-forwarding all the way to the next Christmas. While I found this to be a great exploration for understanding her goals and growth, and how she would come to terms many months later with the difficulties in the story, this wasn't the right ending for the finished book. Regardless, I don't consider that writing wasted time or effort.

Nothing is a waste here. Choose one ending and play with it. What are some settings from earlier in the story that you could bring back at this point? What are the most important loose ends to tie up? Focus on those and allow yourself to make a mistake or two with your ending. Chances are, the mistakes will teach you something you need to know to make your main character more fully formed earlier in your book. These explorations will also help you find that perfect ending later.

So don't spend time judging your ending now. Spend your time writing. You've gotten this far. The fat lady is waiting in the wings, warming up her vocal cords.

Now get to work!

DAY 29 SIMPLE TASK

If you haven't already, make clear how your character has become a new person. The character has gained skills, understanding, and insights about the world. The character may even be more compassionate, particularly for people who suffer the hardship he or she has just survived.

Today, find a way for your main character to help or enhance another character's life with this newfound heart and knowledge.

DAY 30

I want to try it to see what it's like and see what my stuff looks like when I take it from inception to completion.

— Charlie Kaufman

Today is a day for gratitude. Who are the people who have supported you through this month? Who are the people who have helped make you into the tenacious and dedicated type of person who can write an entire novel in a month? Make a point of thanking these people. Bake them a cake. Give them presents. Even if you never attempt writing another novel in a month (though I'll bet you will!), I'm sure this is only the start of the amazing things you'll take on and accomplish, and those same supportive people will continue to be there by your side.

And, of course, be thankful for one more thing: it's over. You're done. You don't have to open this document or look at this draft for at least a couple of weeks. Longer if you want.

But before you go, there's one more thing I'd like you to do today. I'd like you to call your muse all the derogatory names you can think of.

Because you know what? You did this without his or her help. You really did!

Sometimes when you write a novel you rely on your muse's help; I get that. But when you write a novel in thirty days? You don't have time for your muse to stroll in when he or she feels like it and wants to help. Muses are fickle. You really can't depend on them.

This was all you, baby!

You should be very proud of yourself. I'm proud of you.

You should have something ready to reward yourself with after today's writing because not everyone does this. In fact, few people in this world have the perseverance to stay on task with a creative venture the way you have.

One more writing session, and then congratulations!

Take your time and enjoy it!

DAY 30 SIMPLE TASK

This is it — the last writing session! In some ways, the last day is the most important day of all. Here are some things to focus on:

Does your main character end with a sense of hope in some area of life? Perhaps reflect on the ways the character has changed or improved.

Does your story have a feeling of forward momentum? Even if you don't plan to write a sequel, it's important to leave the reader with a sense that your characters' lives will continue to be full and exciting.

Have you reached 50,000 words? If not, I encourage you to write as long as you need to today. If you've written the ending, write additional scenes that you may be able to place earlier in the story. Remember, nothing is wasted. It all helps you get to know your characters, and 50,000 words is a good starting place for a strong revision. It's also a good life practice to push yourself to achieve your goals.

Then, your final task today is to prepare an appropriate celebratory snack! Scour your cupboards or your local store for whatever will signify a celebration for you: champagne, chocolate, guacamole, or anything special.

Congratulations on an enormous accomplishment! Few

people will understand how much dedication this took, but I understand.

Now...take a breather. Whether it's a week or a year, take some time to let your brain relax. When you feel ready, and only after you've had a proper break, turn to part 3 in this book, which is specifically designed to take you through the revision process of your brand-new treasure!

THE BASIC PLAN (CHEAT SHEET)

This is a cheat sheet (or recap) that you may want to look at if you decide to use this guide for a second, third, or fourth time. It is only meant as a quick reminder of each daily task. Please see the individual days for the full explanation.

Day 1 — First setting shown. Main character's (MC) need or desire shown.

Day 2 — Focus on genre.

Day 3 — Introduce a selfless act. Add a symbol, image, or icon.

Day 4 — Make MC's need universal.

Day 5 — Visualize story with actors and music to spark creativity.

Day 6 — Show MC's big weakness. Who is he/she hurting? Establish moral dilemma.

Day 7 — Small tensions lead to an inciting incident. MC can't go back.

Day 8 — Launch act II.

Day 9 — Subplot launched. Another character's desires shown.

Day 10 — Another image introduced. Another question raised.

Day 11 — MC dreams for a day or introduce a terrible event.

Day 12 — Character comparisons.

Day 13 — Renewed understanding of comparisons and strengths/weaknesses.

Day 14 — New goal. New mantra.

Day 15 — Reintroduce image.

Day 16 — Make opponent stronger (thereby making MC stronger).

Day 17 — MC shows smarts or skill in some strong way.

Day 18 — MC shows desperation. Your MC's trust is broken.

Day 19 — Betrayal of someone on MC's side. Object of hope taken out of reach.

Day 20 — MC's dream is almost gone, but MC shows small sign of strength.

Day 21 — Latest reveal gives MC smarts to make a new good plan.

Day 22 — MC trains or improves in some way.

Day 23 — Dark night of the soul.

Day 24 — Launch act III.

Day 25 — Recognize fatal flaw.

Day 26 — MC overcomes opponent.

Day 27 — Check momentum.

Day 28 — Show theme.

Day 29 — MC uses newfound character traits to help/enhance others.

Day 30 — Forward momentum and hope.

Part Three

AFTER THE DRAFT

REVISION
TECHNIQUES

Have you taken some time away from your fast draft? If not, do that now. I'll wait.

After you finish your fast draft, one of my strongest recommendations is to take a break before revising. Your brain needs time to switch over from micro- to macrothinking. You need to gain a little perspective and see the big picture. Otherwise, you may end up just tinkering with comma placement and spelling during revisions and not really making the book better.

To get that necessary perspective, you need to come at the manuscript with fresh eyes. I recommend a minimum of two weeks away from the draft you've just written. I honestly don't think you can take too much time away from a draft, but you can take too little. I've taken months and even years away from drafts. This helped tremendously in seeing how the book's pacing moved from a reader's point of view. To get this added perspective, you may only need a couple of weeks, or you may feel you need longer.

Feel free to skip over to another project. Remember that

shiny new idea that came to you during your last week of drafting? Play around with that one for a few weeks. Make some outline notes, and do some free writing in a character's voice. If you have another book that needs revising, focus on that, so that your brain shifts into revision mode. For me, this shift takes about two weeks of patient, diligent working, so now I usually opt to work on "fun writing" for a short time. If you still feel some writerly momentum, focus it on another project and continue carving out daily writing time, so that your writing remains a priority and a habit. You may, of course, take a complete break from writing and revising during this time.

Once you've taken some time away, read this chapter. My main aim isn't to provide a comprehensive guide for revisions, which would be its own book. My goal is to give you enough advice to get started. For more direction with your revision, two books I highly recommend are Kate Messner's *Real Revision* and Cheryl Klein's *Second Sight*.

However, if at the end of your fast-drafting month, you're feeling discouraged about your story and feel it may not be worth revising, I encourage you to take a much longer break before deciding. With one recent fast draft, it was all I could do to make myself write to the end because I was convinced it was falling apart about halfway through and I didn't know how to fix it. But I put thoughts about revisions out of my mind and pushed through on the fast draft. After writing "The End," I needed a full year before I even wanted to look at that book, but when I did, I was amazed at how engaging it was! It felt like reading someone else's book. I didn't remember much of what I had written during fast-drafting a year before, so all the twists and turns really took me by surprise. I couldn't put it down! I now think of this as one of my strongest books.

So if you're feeling discouraged, don't think about your fast draft for six months or a year. Then come back and read your draft. You don't have to commit to revising it if you still don't want to, but take a few hours to see if you can mine anything valuable out of it.

Then, when you're ready to revise, consider using the following revision techniques. They are presented in the order that I usually work through them, but feel free to work with whatever ones inspire you.

Finally, while some of the following revision techniques include a partial or full read-throughs of your manuscript, if you've taken a really long break after writing, you might consider reading the whole thing once to refresh your mind before attempting revisions.

The "Why Should I Care?" Test

My initial test is on the first page of my manuscript. I go through each sentence and try to think like a new reader. As objectively as possible I ask myself, "Why should I care?"

If you can't think of why someone would care, consider how you can add more conflict to the opening situation. Can you immediately introduce a character whose personality will grind against your main character's? Are there questions you can raise? Is there a way to make your main character more likable and someone the reader will care about right off the bat? Focus on your first two pages, adding questions and conflict, but go over your first three chapters with this in mind.

It's very possible that your initial pages and your first chapters are too heavily weighted with backstory. Do you feel like you need to explain a lot to the reader before the action can get started? Instead, open right into an action scene and explain some of the backstory as you go, or even later. I almost always have to take chunks of backstory and rearrange or cut them as I revise a fast draft.

In particular, how strong is the first line? Is it smart, witty, or powerful, and does it tie into your theme? Review your theme wordle for more inspiration. If you're stuck for a perfect first line, don't stress. I've had times when I've been on my tenth revision before that perfect first line has come to me.

Finally, ask some people to be your early readers; see below for advice on choosing these people. Send them the first three chapters. Ask them, "When do you start to care about my main character and his or her situation?" This is important information. If readers don't start to care until the end of chapter 3 (or at all), you have a problem. Readers need to be invested in your character's life and plight as soon as possible, and at least by the end of the first chapter.

The Big Picture — Main Plot vs. Subplots

After passing the "Why should I care?" test, the next thing I look at is the overall arc of my novel. Do a read-through of your entire draft if you haven't already. Is the main plot clear? Does the main character have a major goal, a major obstacle, and worthy character traits to overcome that obstacle? After facing the obstacle, does the main character have some kind of satisfying resolution, whether the character achieves his or her original goal or not?

Usually most of the above comes naturally to me. If you have a character readers care about, chances are you'll care about the character enough to show his or her strengths through trials. However, if the main plot is not clear, nail down what is missing. Could you work to make your main character's goal more apparent? Perhaps have the character state it outright. How can you make that goal more universal? Or perhaps conflict is lacking. Can your character face a bigger obstacle? Or can you ambush your character with a series of obstacles? If the ending isn't working in your plot arc, consider whether your character's outcome is truly what he or she needs to move on and grow as a person. If the character reached his or her goal, perhaps that's not the best answer for this particular journey. Try having him or her discover a better alternative than the original goal.

The part that doesn't come as naturally for me is making sure that subplots fill in the empty spaces of the story arc. During early revisions, once the main plot is in place, the subplots become my focus. How do you go about creating and fleshing out subplots? Study your antagonist and secondary characters.

If you feel as though your story moves too quickly through the main character's journey, a good way to spend some extra time along the way without losing momentum is to create engaging subplots. This will also help you fully explore your secondary characters. Each one of your secondary characters should be on his or her own journey, with his or her own set of problems and obstacles.

Not all of these need to be shown in the novel, of course. But during revision, I usually err on the side of showing too many people's stories. Later, you can always cut back on the less engaging ones, or the ones that aren't tied closely to the main plot.

If you don't know some of your secondary characters' plights, now is the time to discover them. Return to chapter 3 and review the "Creating Secondary Characters" section (page 34); also, do the exercises in the section "Take Time to Get to Know Your Characters" (page 42). Do this for every secondary character and then look for motivations and character qualities in your secondary characters' lives that could easily tie in to your main plot. Each secondary character should also relate to your themes. How do they feel about or react to these thematic topics? Ideally, secondary characters will relate to themes in a different way than your main character does.

Once you've found some opposing traits and motivations for a secondary character, create a satisfying subplot by giving that secondary character three scenes throughout your novel to explore and overcome his or her obstacle or relate to the theme. Add more scenes if you like, keeping in mind that you don't want your subplots to take over from the main plot, but less than three scenes may not allow for a thorough exploration of the subplot or a satisfying resolution. Keep in mind that these scenes should be tied to the main character and his or her journey in some way.

List of Scenes

Just as you did when planning for your fast draft (see chapter 7), make a list of scenes. However, this list includes only those scenes that *did* make it into your fast draft, whether you preconceived them prior to writing or not.

As in chapter 7, for each scene, list the main event, the function of the scene, the setting, the characters involved, and finally the outcome of the scene.

Mark a star beside any scene that doesn't have a strong function in the story. Especially now, every single scene in your novel needs a purpose and should give your story forward momentum.

Watch especially for transition scenes, ones that only serve to take your character from one situation or location to another. Do you need that transition, or could you simply jump to the start of the next scene?

Cut any scenes without a strong function (and add any important background information to other scenes), or revise that scene so it's more life changing or revealing for your main character.

Ask the following questions regarding each questionable scene:

- Can you add higher stakes that relate to your main character's goal or desire?
- Can the character get either closer to or farther from his or her goal?
- Can any relationships irrevocably change through this scene?

Finally, go back to the original list of scenes you created during planning. Are there any scenes that you didn't write that you wish had made it into your draft? If you think they would still serve your story, making either the conflicts or characterizations stronger, add these scenes to the story now.

Treat Your Novel Like a Screenplay

I've learned so much about writing in general from screenwriting teachers. In Additional Resources, I highly recommend Blake Snyder's *Save the Cat!* This is officially a screenwriting resource, but it's incredibly helpful for writers of any kind of fiction.

For any scenes or chapters that seem rambling or weak and could use some tightening or a better pace, try this dialogue technique.

Create a new Word document for that scene, and give it a new name so it doesn't get confused with the completed draft.

In a few sentences, write a brief scene introduction indicating the basic setting and placement of characters.

Then, cut everything except for the dialogue.

Basically, by cutting everything but dialogue, you're turning your novel into a screenplay. How does it read now? Keep your eye open for anything that wouldn't make sense to the reader without further explanation. For these spots, add some basic direction and use stronger dialogue to convey what your reader needs to know.

This technique will help make your dialogue sharper, stronger, and more revealing, so you don't "tell" the reader so much of what is happening in a scene.

Finally, combine this screenwriting version with your original version. Add your new stronger dialogue to your full draft and cut any description or explanation that seemed extraneous in your screenwriting version. Read it over. Is the scene stronger?

Do this with any scene in your book that feels like it needs some tightening and strength.

Focus on Pacing

To decide if the story's pacing is working well, writers often need opinions from readers. Because we know our characters better than any reader will and we know what exciting story events are coming, it can be difficult to have perspective, especially during slow-moving sections. However, prior to getting outside feedback, there are a few ways to check and adjust your pacing on your own. Are any of your chapters overly long? Could they be broken up? How about scenes? Do some scenes early in your book ramble on for twenty or more pages, while some only last a page or two?

Short scenes, chapters, and even sentences can add to the tension and intensity of the climax and to other sections as well. But are there wild changes in sentence, scene, and chapter length that could read as erratic? Smooth these out as much as you can.

When you feel like you're ready for outside opinions, I recommend you find at least three readers who will comment specifically on your book's pacing; see below for more on selecting readers. Personal opinion certainly makes a difference in this area. If one reader is an expert in some aspect of your story world, he or she may be riveted by your detailed descriptions, while those same scenes may put other readers to sleep. Ultimately, you want to know: Do your readers agree that a certain section of the book moves slowly and makes them eager to skim and move on? Do they find that the ending, or any section, moves too fast, so they become confused or need more information?

Focus on Theme

As I mention during planning, the process of writing a draft is often necessary to nail down your story's theme. Now that you've finished your fast draft, is that true for you? Do you have a stronger sense of your story's central themes?

Either way, return to and revise your visual theme wordle. Which words or phrases now ring more true than others? Circle those. What words or phrases would you now like to add? Write those in and circle them.

Then, take the most important words or phrases (usually no more than three) and form them into a sentence. Write that sentence on a note card and keep it beside your computer while revising. Then, as you keep revising the book, continue revising this thematic sentence to reflect it. Can you make this theme clearer throughout your book? Perhaps it should be stated outright. Think again of *The Wizard of Oz*. I'll bet you can guess at the theme because it's stated outright several times: There's no place like home. How can you make your theme more obvious?

Or, on the other hand, you may find that the theme is too prominent in your fast draft. If you get to the end of your read-through and you feel the narrative is too preachy or heavy-handed because of your focus on theme, it's likely because your plot is lacking and underdeveloped. A strong theme needs a strong plot.

A strong theme + a weak plot = a preachy tale.

If this is the case, I encourage you to return to working on strengthening your character's motivations and the obstacles that will come between your character and his or her goals.

Selecting Outside Readers during Revisions

As you revise your novel, it's important to get feedback from others. These early readers are critical for providing an outside perspective on what's working and what isn't in your story. As writers, we see our fully realized stories — what we intend the story to be — whenever we read it, and this often makes it difficult to judge how much of our intended story and character qualities make it from our brains onto the page. Without feedback, you might not realize that all of your diligent revisions are not fixing your story's actual problems.

Before you seek outside opinions, however, it's important to diagnose and even try to solve the issues to some degree on your own. Know what you think the problems might be, and in a couple of scenes try to fix them. In particular, revise your early pages using the guidance in this chapter: ask the "Why should I care" question, check the pacing, strengthen dialogue, ensure the main plot is clear, and if warranted, add exciting subplots.

Then look for new readers who can give you a fresh perspective on your story. You can never have too many readers when you're revising a book. The trick is to find the *right* readers for you.

Having danced professionally with a dance troupe for most of my life, I'm no stranger to harsh criticism. I admit, writing critiques feel a little more personal, since I feel like so much of my private thought process comes out on the page. But still, I look for people who won't mince words and will tell me as clearly and bluntly as possible what they think.

This takes a thick skin. Even then, criticism still stings. If you feel you need a gentler hand, that's okay! But it's important to know what *you* need before looking for help, and then tell each person very clearly what type and tone of feedback you're looking for. The process of critiquing has been known to ruin friendships, as well as a writer's passion for his or her book, and these are worse outcomes than not seeking advice at all.

For these reasons, I caution against asking family and friends for feedback, at least initially. Those close to you may also read subtext into your book that's not there, or see the characters, especially the main character, as being an extension of you, which can hinder objective feedback.

If you don't know where to find objective readers, try Twitter, Facebook, or www.CritiqueCircle.com. These are all great resources to find people willing to read and offer feedback. You should not need to pay for feedback, especially at this early stage, but unfortunately, finding the best readers is a process of trial and error. Look for people who read, and enjoy, the genre you're writing in. If you receive feedback that does not address the questions you asked (more on that below), or that comes across more harshly or more sugarcoated than you want, first reevaluate what you asked for from the reader. Were you clear in what you were looking for? If you were, and that reader did not give you the type of feedback you were after, that person may not be the best reader for you. Thank him or her, because reading and offering feedback takes time and effort, but look for other readers for next time. It has taken me years to find the best readers for me and my work, and I value them highly.

Tell your readers up front what you are looking for. If you want an opinion on the full book, tell them that. If you want them looking only at specific issues, like pacing, or only certain sections, like the first three chapters, tell them that, too. Also, if you're in early revisions, you might want to specify that you don't want readers to focus on spelling and grammatical errors. Some readers can't help but point out smaller errors, which is fine, as long as they focus on the big picture as well.

I usually send out specific questions along with my manuscript. I always ask readers when they started to care. I usually ask them to keep their eyes open for boring bits, parts they wanted to skim, and any plot points or character motivations they didn't understand or find believable. I also like to ask what their favorite scene was and what parts of the story they found to be the most engaging.

If you've asked them to read the whole book, quiz readers about how they felt about the climax. Were they riveted? Why or why not? Did your character do something unforgivable leading up to the climax? Is your main character not challenged enough (which may make your reader blasé about the outcome)?

Ultimately, aim to have at least three readers read the entire story. This should give you enough feedback to overhaul your book in ways that will make it infinitely better and more engaging. I caution against any heavy revising based on a single reader's feedback. Unless that feedback strongly resonates with you, I suggest seeking at least a second opinion, as all feedback is subjective.

As you scrutinize feedback, you will sometimes need to weigh conflicting opinions. Make sure you don't listen to only the positive feedback, pat yourself on the back, and ignore any criticisms. This feels better to your self-esteem, but it won't improve your writing. If one reader loves a scene that another reader is bored silly by, don't discount the bored reader. You might be tempted to dismiss the negative reader (perhaps because he or she is not part of your target audience), but that person is identifying something that could be problematic, and it doesn't serve you to ignore it.

Instead, it's more effective to really study the person's criticisms and look for ways to fix the issues while keeping all the great stuff that your other reader loved. All the while, of course, you want to maintain the integrity of your story. Revisions can be tricky business!

After one round of initial revisions, then reader feedback, and then more revisions, you may be tempted to consider your work done. I recommend going through this process with at least two more sets of three readers. It may be a temptation to use the same readers, especially if they were very helpful the first time, but I encourage you to find new readers who can look at your book with fresh eyes. Even though you see the changes you made during revision as drastic, if the overall arc of your story remains, it will still read like the same story to previous readers, and it may tire them.

Even when people read with a critical eye, they're still individuals. Chances are, some will still find various problems even after many revisions. But ideally those problems will get smaller, and when you're getting *mostly* great feedback and multiple readers are saying they couldn't put your book down — that's when you know it's probably ready to send to publishing professionals.

Conclusion

I hope this guide has been helpful to you, and I hope you will use it again and again to help fast-draft new novels. If there's anything I haven't covered that you wish I had, please drop me a note at d@denisejaden.com. I'd love to hear about it, and I would be happy to add regular updates and addendums on my blog at denisejaden.blogspot.com.

I'd also love to hear about your experiences fast-drafting — good or bad. Please drop me a note and let me know how it went for you!

ADDITIONAL RESOURCES

The Anatomy of Story by John Truby (New York: Faber & Faber, 2008)

This is a thorough guide to story, character, and plotting, but especially to the basic structure of your plot. The book breaks down every detail of story structure. Truby uses plenty of examples from well-known literature.

Bird by Bird by Anne Lamott (New York: Anchor Books, 1995)

Though we often work alone, writing doesn't have to be lonely. Lamott understands the writer's psyche and has a great ability to reveal our similarities.

The Creative Habit by Twyla Tharp (New York: Simon & Schuster, 2006)

Are you still having trouble getting it in gear to get your daily writing done? This is a great resource to help you prepare for success.

The First Five Pages by Noah Lukeman (New York: Touchstone, 2000)

If you're having trouble with your beginning, or figuring out exactly where to begin, this is a great resource.

No Plot? No Problem! by Chris Baty (San Francisco: Chronicle Books, 2004)

From the creator of National Novel Writing Month (NaNoWriMo, www.nanowrimo.org), this is a great motivational companion for people who want to complete a fast draft with a little more of the fly-by-the-seat-of-one's-pants method.

Real Revision by Kate Messner (Portland, ME: Stenhouse Publishers, 2011)

Another great companion resource for revising, including wonderfully creative exercises.

Save the Cat! by Blake Snyder (Studio City, CA: Michael Weise Productions, 2005)

While this is officially a book for screenwriters, it applies to any storytellers who hope to sell their work. Snyder breaks down effective stories in a simple and concise manner that anyone can understand. His "Beat Sheet" will show you what may be missing from your stories. An indispensable resource.

Second Sight by Cheryl Klein (Saline, MI: Asterisk Books, 2011)

A behind-the-scenes look at editing and revision from a professional who knows her stuff. A great companion resource for when you reach the revision stage.

Writing the Breakout Novel by Donald Maass (Cincinnati: Writer's Digest Books, 2001)

This is a great resource for learning about tension and conflict. Is your pace dipping? Does your book have lagging problem spots? This book is for you.

ACKNOWLEDGMENTS

My first thanks go to God for giving me an introspective and philosophical mind. Often there is no place I'd rather be than inside my head, and whether through fiction or nonfiction, I'm grateful that there are people to help me get my thoughts from my head into a coherent and cohesive book.

Thanks always to my family and friends for all their ongoing support of me and my writing. Thanks especially to my husband, Ted, and son, Teddy, for bearing with me through my process of learning how to fast-draft.

Thanks to Shana Silver for introducing me to the idea of fast-drafting, and to Catherine Knutsson, Tara Quigley, and Michelle Humphrey for their help with various early drafts of this manuscript.

Also thanks to Jason Gardner, Georgia Hughes, Monique Muhlenkamp, and the rest of the editorial, marketing, and publicity team at New World Library for helping me get this book polished and out into the world. Thanks to Jeff Campbell for his insightful editorial advice for this manuscript.

My heartfelt thanks to Chris Baty, Lindsey Grant, Chris Angotti, Grant Faulkner, and the rest of the team who have been instrumental in bringing the NaNoWriMo November writing challenge to life each year.

And last, but certainly not least, thank you to my #wip madness/March Madness friends who encourage me and cheer me on all year long.

It is no small thing to make a writer feel like they are not alone in the world. Thank you all so much!

ABOUT THE AUTHOR

Denise Jaden has been fast-drafting since 2007, when she wrote the first draft of her debut novel, *Losing Faith*, in twenty-one days during the NaNoWriMo writing challenge. She has participated in (and won) the NaNoWriMo challenge each year since, and she now runs a secondary fast-drafting challenge on her blog each March at denisejaden.blogspot.com. Her second novel from Simon & Schuster, *Never Enough*, was released in 2012, and a group of companion stories, *Never Enough Stories*, is available for free at Smashwords.com. *Writing with a Heavy Heart: Using Grief and Loss to Stretch Your Fiction* was her first nonfiction work for writers. She loves teaching groups of writers of all ages and infusing them with confidence to attempt their own fast drafts.

Denise lives just outside Vancouver, Canada, with her personal-trainer husband and her ten-year-old fast-drafting son. Find out more about Denise and her writing online at www.denisejaden.com or on Twitter: @denisejaden.